WHEN NOTHING WORKS
TRY DOING
NOTHING

How Learning to Let Go Will
Get You Where You Want to Go

The author of this book does not dispense medical advice or prescribe the use of any technique as a form of treatment for physical, emotional, or medical problems without the advice of a physician, either directly or indirectly. The intent of the author is only to offer information of a general nature to help you in your quest for emotional and spiritual well-being. In the event you use any of the information in this book for yourself, which is your constitutional right, the author and the publisher assume no responsibility for your actions.

Library of Congress Control Number: 2014912762

Kinslow, Frank J
When Nothing Works Try Doing Nothing: How Learning to Let Go Will Get You Where You Want to Go /Dr. Frank J Kinslow. – 1ˢᵗ edition
ISBN 978-0-9844264-2-3 1. Mind and body. 2. Awareness. 3. Success. 4. Natural healing.

To George Land and Beth Jarman
for their support and guidance,
but most of all their inspiration

and

To my wife Martina
for her encouragement to write this book
– but, most of all, for her smile

and

To "The Guys" --
Dick Bisbing, Dick Harris, and Rod Trier
for fifty-five years of friendship.
Thanks guys, for everything.

CONTENTS

PREFACE

To the New Reader

If you are not familiar with my previous works, the book you hold in your hand is meant for you. I am certain you will find reading it enjoyable – but that is the least of it. Even though the teaching is logical and draws on scientific research, the language I use is simple and conversational. I use plenty of analogies and anecdotes, so don't worry about getting lost. The techniques that you will learn are easy and immediately effective. They are also scientific – by which I mean that they are reproducible: if you follow the steps, you get the results. That doesn't mean that the techniques are dry and lifeless. Quite the contrary; you will find them enlivening and even inspiring.

Almost every self-help book brags that the knowledge within is "life changing". We read this proclamation on the jackets of diet books, exercise books, financial books, books about relationships, books about alternative medicine, etc. – and in the strictest sense they are right. Losing weight or improving your relationship *does* change your life in some way. But I am going to make this statement

– and I almost hesitate to do so because the phrase has been overused, if not abused. When I tell you that this book will change your life, I am referring not to a specific area like relationships, finances, health, spirituality, and so on. The understanding you get from reading this book and the experience you receive from practicing its simple techniques will change every level of your life, from your spiritual to your financial, from your mind into your body, from your sense of self out into the global community. I can say this because we are not focusing on a *part* of you. This book introduces you to the wholeness that is you, how to instantly access that wholeness, and then how to encourage its infusion into every aspect of your being and becoming.

The entire book should be taken as a single unit. Each chapter builds on the last. Each experience also builds on the previous one. Knowledge has two parts to it: understanding and experience. Knowledge has no value unless understanding supports experience, which then supports further understanding, which supports further experience and so on. As you complete each chapter of this book, your knowledge about who you are, your inner essence, will grow deeper and broader. You will begin with the simplest experience of "no thinking", showing you what lies beyond your thoughts. It takes only seconds to have this perception and instantly you will see the results in both your body and your mind. When you turn the last page of this small book you will know why humanity has become so destructive, and why suffering is so prevalent. You will understand who you are, where you are, which direction you need to go, and how to get there. And you will know this not because I told you but from your own animated experience.

I strongly suggest that you do not skip ahead, but read each page in its turn, practice each experience before moving on to the next. Don't look at this book as work, but as play. Read it in a spirit of adventure. Be easy and take your time with the experiences. Practice the last experience as you continue reading, then practice the next one. The second-to-last chapter, Chapter 15 – On Becoming Fully Human: 90 Days of EuStillness, will give you suggestions on how to integrate what you have learned into your daily routine. I definitely want to encourage you have fun with this 90-day EuStillness package. It is almost effortless and you will be quite bowled over by the way your life has changed after 90 days. After all, how many 90-day periods have you had in your life so far? Just think of what one more 90-day period will mean to you in terms of health, happiness, and success.

This book is a reflection of my consciousness. I want you to feel that I wrote this book for you, that I am speaking directly to you. I wrote this book in EuStillness, the heightened state of harmony that you will soon be learning about. This teaching is not traditional. It is not a collection of philosophies, facts, and anecdotes. In essence, what you learn is not coming from outside of you. With just a little guidance, you will discover that the knowledge has always been contained within you, waiting for you to discover it and tease it out into the light. If you begin to feel inner quietness and a sense of well-being as you read, then the book is no longer paper and print but has become a living embodiment of the teaching. In time, with a little practice, you will find that everything in your life will become the living embodiment of the wholeness that you are.

To Those Familiar with My Previous Works

If you are familiar with my previous works, you will find *When Nothing Works Try Doing Nothing: How Learning to Let Go Will Get You Where You Want to Go* both familiar and innovative. The philosophy of doing nothing and "not trying" are still very much in evidence in this work. The emphasis of this book is on the science and art of EuStillness. If you have been practicing Quantum Entrainment then you can easily substitute the EuStillness Technique for QE. The simple shift will add depth to your practice and will accelerate and amplify the effects of QE. Every technique in this book is new and original. I am sure you will have a lot of fun with all of them and will be surprised at the clarity and depth your practice will assume.

Whether you are fresh to the idea that "doing nothing gets things done" and "not trying builds the foundation for dynamic activity" or are a seasoned veteran of several years and many miracles, I can guarantee you this: reading this book and following its instruction will profoundly impact not only you, your body, mind, and spirit, but will have a harmonizing and healing influence on your family and friends, those who support you, those who oppose you, perfect strangers, pets, plants ... well, you get the idea.

Whether you are a new reader or long time QE-er, I am certain this book will unravel deeper mysteries long contemplated. I am very passionate about the knowledge within, and anxious to share it with you. When you turn the last page I am confident you will share my passion.

Frank Kinslow
Sarasota, Florida

CHAPTER 1

THE ART OF NOTHING

*"How beautiful it is to do nothing,
and then to rest afterward."*

~SPANISH PROVERB

Picture a world where you are following your innermost desires, doing the work that you are naturally drawn to do and love. It dovetails perfectly with your talents and interests. Your work regenerates you rather than tiring you out. Time flies by almost too quickly. Like the flickering splinters of a lit sparkler, creativity burns within you. You are self-motivated, take pride in your work, and feel like you are a cohesive and contributing part of a grander plan. You are complete. In essence you are living in accord with your natural talents and interests, at one within yourself and with your environment.

Now zoom out so that you are looking down on a city of people just like you. Each is a productive and prodigious part of a grander plan. With little conscious effort, each soul supports the other joyfully and with selfless purpose.

Conflicts still exist but are resolved from a level of creative exuberance, joy, and playfulness. Distorting emotions and aberrant behavior are all but nonexistent. This city is not a place of individual minds, methodologies, and self-serving agendas. It is an entity unto itself. It is alive, a whole being, more than the sum of its parts, a vibrant reflection of the contentment and creativity of its inhabitants.

Now zoom out further so that you are looking down on the whole Earth, that liquid blue marble spinning silently, powerfully on its axis. Know that every individual of every city of every country is living in perfect harmony within Nature. We all have this vision of Utopia inside us. It came with us when we burst into this world and drew that first blazing breath of life into our lungs. It was there in childhood before we were taught our limitations. Then it was set aside, sequestered in the dungeons within, those dark places where we chain our most animated dreams until they tire. And there they slumber in the darkness, waiting. It takes but a single shard of sunlight to scatter the darkness and reawaken even our deepest dreams.

This is what you will learn in this book. You will discover the sunlight that already abides within you. This is not something you must acquire. You do not need to train or travel. You already have everything you need to see that light. You need only look in the direction of the sun, and memory becomes living reality.

We have so much potential. Don't you think so? My goodness, but what we can do. I could list the usual things like putting a man on the moon, the pyramids, heavier-than-air flight, and so on and so forth. Compared to the other species that co-habit this Earth with us, our progress has been phenomenal. And we are continuing to grow, in so many ways, exponentially.

We are progressing by leaps and bounds. Look how far we have come in just the last 100 years. If you were to visit a city in the United States at the turn of the 20th century you would find people of the day heating by coal or wood, lighting by candle or gas, local locomotion by foot or horse, and the nightly contents of the chamber pot emptied each morning at the family outhouse. Poverty, illiteracy, social prejudice and injustice, and religious intolerance were the norm. But all that has changed dramatically.

The United States is the quintessential rags-to-riches story, but it doesn't look like it is moving toward a happy ending. That is what this book is about, happy endings, not for just the United States but for every individual in every country, from every race, spiritual orientation, educational background, financial standing, and level of personal health, on this Earth. Big words, I know, but what if I could actually back them up? Would the chance to realize your personal Utopia be worth the time it takes to read this little book? If I am wrong, at the very least you can have a good laugh at the ravings of a madman. But if I am right …

We have vision and imagination and good intentions. We have come a long way from hunting and gathering, and still there is so much more to grow. But despite our overwhelming progress, we don't seem to be satisfied. We seem to have bottomed out in the contentment department. But what is it that we are really trying to do? What is our endgame? When everything is said and done, what will we have … who will we be?

We have the survival thing nailed down. Let me amend that statement. We are experts at basic survival. Shelter and food and procreation are, for us, no-brainers. Don't get me wrong. There are still pockets of poverty and strife, where one's very life breath is threatened on a daily basis – but that is the result of local circumstances and not for lack of know-how. Yes, we are masters of basic survival, but oddly enough the survival of our species is in doubt. That's because we were meant for a grander good.

Don't you feel it? Don't you feel that something seems to be missing, something basic and deeply primordial? Haven't you ever asked yourself, "Is this all there is to life?" You may have asked this question in a quiet moment of reflection but then trampled it under foot on your way out the door to buy a bigger, brighter widget, find a sympathetic ear to bend, or indulge any of a plethora of electronic diversions to keep that tormenting question from resurfacing. It makes us uncomfortable because we don't know what source gave birth to that question. More importantly, we don't know how to satisfy it. But it is vital, not only to our mental health but for the survival of our species, that we find the source of this dis-ease.

In the short time that we spend together between the covers of this book I will offer you a revolutionary perspective on the current and precarious position that clearly defines why, despite our nearly infinite potential, we are foundering on the precipice of destruction. This new perspective is, in part, a rearrangement of existing research and theories that has created a new vision. It's like rearranging letters of an old word to create a new word with greater depth of meaning. For instance, when you read the word "dog", an image may pop into your mind of a hairy, four-legged, tail-wagging friend who enjoys the simple pleasures of life with you. Rearrange the letters d-o-g to spell g-o-d and you are confronted with the most profound mystery of life.

Knowledge is complete only when understanding is supported by experience. I will provide you both. Understanding what is wrong has little value unless you also learn how to fix it. This is particularly exciting as I have discovered a simple and natural process that has immediate results. What results? Why, I'm so glad you asked.

I have found a way to free your mind from the influence of negative emotions and thinking. Now, before you throw it into a heap with all of the other positive thinking, anti-judgment systems hear me out. What I offer you is uniquely and profoundly different. Traditional positive thinking systems require that you, well ... Think positive. They tell you that if you can think positive then positive things will come to you. Most people find that this approach takes a great deal of effort to perpetuate and time to realize, with a high incidence of failure. In fact, recent neurological research indicates that a positive mental attitude is more the result of the individual's natural make-up than manufactured happiness. Thinking positive thoughts has very little *lasting* effect on the psychophysiological structure of the individual.

The process that I discovered does not require that you envision a positive outcome, think positive thoughts, or generate positive emotions. It does not require belief or faith or any peculiar talent or skill. Nor does it require affirmations or intentions or a vivid imagination from which to build your detailed utopian future. All of these efforts take place in your mind. Calling on a distressed mind to fix itself is a lot like asking the fox to guard the hen house. It rarely ends up the way we think it should. To fix a broken mind, you have to step beyond the mind. That is the first thing I will show you how to do.

As you progress through this book, be easy with the concepts and experiences you find within. Some of the concepts may be new to you. Just let them simmer for a while on the back burners of your mind. No need to pressure yourself or struggle to understand everything right away. The experiences you have will fill in the gaps for you. They are simple and create a feeling of welcoming naturalness. Your experiences will support the concepts you learn. You don't need faith or belief. It is necessary that you only follow the instructions and rely on your own experience for verification.

Despite its seemingly esoteric nature, what you are about to learn is scientific and reproducible. I am as eager to teach you this remarkable technique as I expect you are eager to learn. So we will begin the first step of the teaching in the next chapter. After you learn the technique and begin practicing on your own, I will introduce you to the science behind the technique. Then we will look into the science of enlightenment, what it is and how it works. We will see what scientists are saying about it and discuss the actual experiences of people who are enlightened, so that you will recognize those experiences when they appear in you. Together we will explore what it means to become fully human.

I expect you will enjoy this book immensely. It will offer you a simple yet profound message. By the time you finish reading it you will have learned that you are complete just as you are, right now. You will have discovered a secret that has been hiding in plain view. You will realize that your troubles have only come from looking in the wrong direction. It is as if you have been standing on a promontory facing the side of the mountain. I will simply ask you to turn around. From this new perspective, this exalted height will open your vision to greater possibilities and potential. Thread by thread, the mysteries of your life will begin to unravel. You will wonder at the simplicity of it all and take great satisfaction in knowing that you are OK, and will be OK, as understanding replaces confusion and joy replaces consternation.

What does all this flowery talk mean in everyday, nuts and bolts, practical applications? Here are just a few things that you will be able to do when you have finished reading this book:

- Enjoy more success and enjoy your success more
- Begin healing yourself and others in minutes
- Discover where you are, where you need to go, and how to get there
- Find yourself and love what you find
- How to make the right decision
- The negative effects of positive thinking
- Love yourself and find that love in others
- Know what it means to be enlightened
- Begin a 90-day program to decrease discord and increase success
- Have fun

Main Points – Chapter 1

- We humans have vision and imagination and good intentions, but remain discontent.

- Something primordial is missing from our lives.

- Knowledge is complete only when understanding is supported by experience.

- Traditional positive thinking systems require great effort, with a high incidence of failure.

- To fix a broken mind, you have to step outside the mind.

- You are complete just as you are right now.

CHAPTER 2

HOW NOTHING WORKS

*"No matter what I tried, nothing worked.
And then I got it. Nothing works!"*

~FRANK KINSLOW

I know that quoting myself may seem a little self-absorbed, but when I first made this discovery I was totally bowled over by its implications. This single revelation has sparked a revolution that has reduced suffering and improved the quality of life of many, many thousands around the globe. It is why we are meeting here, and I just wanted to share this insight with you.

What I have discovered does not depend on your mind, but on your *awareness*. Do you have awareness? Well of course you do, otherwise you would not be reading this book. You don't have to synthetically generate your awareness like you do with a positive emotion, right? When you are awake you are aware naturally and without effort. So this is our starting point, common everyday awareness.

The next ingredient in this remarkable recipe to re-move suffering and increase success is *perception*. Percep-tion is how you fill your awareness. We perceive through our senses: sight, taste, touch, smell, and hearing. When you see a flower, the image of the flower is thrown onto the retina of your eye. The perception of the flower on the retina is changed into electrical impulses which are trans-mitted to your brain. Your brain translates the electrical impulses into an image of the flower you are looking at. The whole process is automatic and instantaneous.

In this case you would see the flower but without awareness; you would not know that the flower exists. If your eye were a camera then perception would be the pro-cedure of taking the picture – that is, getting the image of the flower through the lens and recorded on the memory card. In this analogy, awareness is the light that makes the whole process possible. Without light there is effectively no image of the flower and therefore no perception of the flower. As far as you are concerned, it does not exist.

There are many shades of awareness. You can be alert, tired, distracted, drugged, etc. If we think of awareness as light, then the different kinds of awareness represent dif-ferent intensities of light. Let's say that the brightest light possible registers 10 on our "light/awareness" scale. Every-day common consciousness would register a 4 or 5 on our scale of 0 to 10. This would be like using your camera to take a picture outdoors on a cloudy day. Depending on the degree of fatigue, awareness would be a 2 or 3. This would be like taking a picture at dusk just after the sun has set. Drugs like alcohol and other depressants would register 0 to 2, and would be like taking a picture at night. A stimu-lant like caffeine will temporarily push our awareness to 6 or 7 followed by rebound fatigue into the 2 to 3 range. This would be like taking a picture with a flash attachment and then having to recharge the battery.

This discovery is a way to perceive the purest awareness, a 10 on our awareness scale. Having the purest awareness is like taking a picture under perfect conditions in full daylight. When we perceive through pure awareness it gives us the truest, most vibrant reflection of life. It frees us from having to struggle to see life clearly. It gives us the best chance for appreciating the world within which we live.

So what is pure awareness? Pure awareness is nothing! At least, as far as your mind is concerned, pure awareness does not exist. That's because it has no form. Like the daylight in our camera analogy, pure awareness is everywhere but we are basically unaware of it. We don't actually see light. We look right through it, don't we? Because light is present we can see the objects it illumines, but light itself remains hidden. So it is with the nothing of pure awareness.

Experience:
The Nothing Technique

Let's take a short pause to enjoy an experience of pure awareness, shall we? All right, sit comfortably where you won't be disturbed for a couple of minutes. All settled in? You can read the instructions into a recorder or have someone read them to you, pausing for 4 to 5 seconds after each sentence. Or you can get the audio download of me guiding you through the *Nothing Technique* in the audio section of the QE Store on the Kinslow System website at: www.KinslowSystem.com/learn.html. Or you can read the instructions all the way through a couple of times and then follow them by memory. OK, here we go ...

The Nothing Technique

Close your eyes and let your mind wander wherever it wants to go. Now become aware of what you are thinking. The content is not important, just know that thoughts are there. Easily watch your thoughts, as if you were watching a movie. Just let your thoughts flow across the screen of your mind. You are looking at your thoughts ... Now easily look past the thoughts and notice that there is nothing there. Continue to be aware of nothing as long as is comfortable. When thoughts begin again, watch them for a while and then again look beyond them, or between them, at nothing. Do this for 2 to 3 minutes.

First, notice how you feel. Is your body more relaxed? Do you feel quieter in your mind? After only 2 to 3 minutes, you are already beginning to reap the benefits of ... Doing nothing! You didn't have to imagine yourself on a tropical beach, sit in a pretzel-like posture and breathe through one nostril, focus your mind on a candle flame or hum a secret sound. Instantly, the moment you switched your awareness from thoughts to nothing, relaxation and inner peace began growing within you. Nothing is the screen onto which your thoughts are projected. As soon as you became aware of just the screen, you left your thoughts behind, didn't you? The next time you are at the movies, take a moment to become aware of the screen behind the movie. The movie screen is always there, but we rarely pay attention to it. Likewise, nothing is always there behind our thoughts.

When you became aware of nothing, you actually cleared your mind of thought! It did not take years of practice, as many have taught. It took you literally seconds to leave thought behind and become aware of the nothing beyond. If you did nothing else but this simple exercise you would have learned a most powerful meditation, which alone would have a marked impact on your life. But there is more; much, much, much more to come.

Now, let me ask you – what is in that nothing? Crazy question? Nothing is nothing, right? Well, as it turns out there is *something* in the nothing. The something that is in nothing is awareness. Not awareness of something like the moon or an apple. This awareness is awareness of nothing. This is what I call pure awareness. Pure awareness is the ground state, the basic stuff of all created things. As you are already beginning to find out, becoming aware of pure awareness is a very good thing to do.

Everything we experience is through pure awareness. Most people don't even know they have pure awareness, much less that it is their essential nature. It is more intimate to us than our families, our jobs, and even our health, for without pure awareness we would have none of these things. It is pure awareness that makes it possible for us to feel, to think, to perceive, and to experience life in all its vibrant beauty. Pure awareness is our very essence.

In our daily life pure awareness has remained hidden. It works behind the scenes, breathing life into life itself. When we become aware of pure awareness, we tune in to the actual lifeblood of creation. When we become aware of pure awareness, we become like it and the mysteries of life unfold before our very eyes. What's that mean to you in practical everyday language? It means you will have more energy, more success, more fun, and more love – and that is just the tip of the iceberg.

In quantum mechanics, pure awareness is loosely analogous to implicate order, the formless non-energy from which all form and energy come. Everything you perceive – raindrops in a puddle, the hum of your refrigerator motor, the reflection of your face in the mirror – every created thing first begins as pure awareness.

Now here's the problem. Your mind is not interested in pure awareness because it cannot directly perceive it. To the mind, pure awareness is nothing. If it cannot perceive pure awareness, then it cannot do what minds love to do: identify, analyze, manipulate, and create something new. So your mind is quickly bored with pure awareness, the very thing that abolishes boredom. What to do?

Enter Eufeeling! Eufeeling is unique in all creation. It has, so to speak, a foot in both worlds. It is both formless pure awareness and the first beautiful expression of pure awareness in your mind. When you look at the water in an ocean, you see that it takes many forms. On the surface there are waves and foam and currents flowing like great rivers. Below the surface the water exhibits a diverse array of temperatures, densities, and clarity. The surface of the ocean can be very volatile, while on the bottom of the ocean the water can be very still. If your mind were an ocean, pure awareness would be the water and Eufeeling would be the different forms that water becomes. Your thoughts would be like the great variety of life-forms that inhabit the ocean.

Let's step out of our ocean analogy for a moment and find out why positive thinking, as it is presently practiced, does not work. We tend to think that negative and positive thoughts are two different conditions of the same perception, just like hot and cold are two different conditions of water. If hot water were considered negative and cold water positive, then all we have to do is add enough cold water to the hot and it will quickly become cold. Some feel that adding enough positive thoughts to a negative perception will turn it into a positive perception, but in reality that model does not work. Those of us who try to overpower a negative perception with positive thoughts are deluding ourselves. It takes a great deal of energy to maintain a positive attitude in a negative situation. It takes virtually no energy at all to perceive a positive situation. In reality a negative perception and a positive perception are not two different conditions of the same perception. In actuality they are two completely different perceptions. They are apples and oranges. Trying to turn apples into oranges by combining the two only makes a mess. Trying to convince yourself that a mess is not a mess is a form of denial that is both damaging and draining.

With this in mind, let's return to our ocean analogy. All life in an ocean is directly dependent on the conditions of the water. A cold-water fish cannot thrive in tropical waters, just as a positive thought cannot thrive in a negative environment. It does not matter how many friends the cold-water fish takes along with him into tropical waters, he still will not prosper. Now, if the cold-water fish were practicing positive thinking, he would try and convince himself that the warm water was actually cold. Despite what his imagination tells him, the reality of living in warm water will continue to work against his every effort to live a productive life. As his quality of life continues to degrade, he will experience more and more discomfort and negativity and he will have to work harder and harder to maintain the cold water illusion. You see?

Sir Walter Scott knew all about this kind of mess when he penned, "Oh what a tangled web we weave when first we practice to deceive." (I know, you think I messed up and should have given Shakespeare the credit for that quote. I used to think that, too.) Who are we deceiving? Why, ourselves, of course.

Here's the point. Negativity has value. It does no good to try and sweep it under the carpet. When you create the illusion of positivity, you miss the possibility of possibility. That's right. While you work hard to maintain the belief that all is right with your world, you miss the possibility of actually improving it. If our cold-water fish did not practice positive thinking or become self-involved with creating intentions of affluence, he would be left with the stark reality that he does not fit in. This realization is his salvation and the first step on the path to tangible positivity.

Both negativity and positivity have their place in this world. This is an absolute reality. If we deny this reality we are living an illusion. Once we recognize how the two, the positive and the negative, work together, magical things begin to happen. We will dive more deeply into that ocean a little later in this book. By the way, this process, which you will soon learn is very easy to do, is far more difficult to talk about and conceptualize than it is to actually do. Just remember, hundreds of thousands of people around the globe do it every day. Soon you will, too.

OK, back to our ocean-is-mind analogy and the idea that awareness of Eufeeling will give us more freedom and fulfillment. To become aware of the different conditions of water like temperature, clarity, etc., you must first become aware of the water itself. If you say to a fish, "Become aware of the water you are swimming in," he will say, "What water?" But if you pluck that fish out of the water and let him experience the air, when he returns to the water he will certainly know it by contrast. All the different conditions of your mind, thoughts, emotions, memories, perceptions, etc., depend on Eufeeling. To become aware of Eufeeling you must first become like the fish out of water. You must experience pure awareness. Once you do that in just the right way, you settle into the great stillness of mind, much like sinking to the very bottom of the ocean. There is an overwhelming collection of scientific research that extols the healthful benefits, physical, mental, emotional, and spiritual, of this Zen-like quiet state of mind. But we are only halfway there. The value of my discovery is realized in two ways: how to instantly experience this great mental stillness and how to stay there even during very vigorous activity. I know this instant access to inner stillness flies in the face of traditional teachings, but you can't argue with results. You may have heard that it takes years of study and arduous practice to experience no-mind, to clear the mind of thought. Up until now, that has been true. However, I have taught people from many different cultures speaking many different languages from many diverse educational, vocational, financial, and spiritual backgrounds – and all, with just a few minutes of direction, were able to gently leave thought behind and experience the simple joy of Eufeeling. Why? It is because awareness of Eufeeling is the birthright of every human on this Earth. Open access to this inner essence, this inner stillness from which creativity, harmony, and healing flow, is a natural extension of our humanness. It is embedded in our genetic code. Illumined souls of every generation have taught us that it is possible. We just didn't know how easy it is.

Main Points – Chapter 2

- Perception is automatic and instantaneous.

- Without awareness there is no perception.

- Pure awareness is our very essence.

- Awareness of pure awareness improves the quality of life.

- Eufeeling is the first beautiful expression of pure awareness in your mind.

- It takes a great deal of energy to maintain a positive attitude in a negative situation.

- Awareness of Eufeeling eliminates negativity instantly and without effort.

- Awareness of Eufeeling is the birthright of every human.

CHAPTER 3

THE EUSTILLNESS
TECHNIQUE:

Where Does It Come From and How Does It Work?

*"If at first the idea is not absurd,
then there is no hope for it."*

~ALBERT EINSTEIN

In a moment we will look more closely at the EuStillness Technique, the reason for this book. But first I would like to give a little background as to its origin. Wherever I travel, I am often asked to tell the story behind the technique. So for those who want to know where this deceptively simple yet decidedly effective technique comes from, I dedicate these next few paragraphs to you.

I discovered this solution to suffering not because I possess supernormal powers of introspection or somehow have connected to the mystic forces of Nature, not at all. Like many remarkable discoveries, it was simply a matter of being in the right place at the right time in the right state of awareness.

It all started in ninth grade during my Latin 101 class. By the time midterm rolled around I was so miserably lost that my teacher, Mrs. Whiteman, a stern disciplinarian with piercing black eyes, confronted me. She informed me that because I thus far had been unable to demonstrate the basics of this dead language I had no possible chance of passing her class. She asked me what I had to say for myself. I wanted to show her that I had learned something in her class by reciting the phrase *ubi sunt virgines* (where are the girls), but thought this might not be the most opportune time to enlighten her, so I just looked at my shoes and mumbled something unintelligible. What I didn't voice was my fear of speaking Latin. After all, the ancient Romans spoke Latin and they are all dead. I am certain that she took my failure as a personal affront to her teaching skills, as if I had set out to sacrifice my GPA just to make her look bad. She told me that I must continue attending class but that I could only read during that hour. I felt like I had been let out of prison! Just show up and read? I suspect she hoped I would continue with my Latin studies and retake her class second semester. Instead I let my imagination explode. I became a member of anthropologist Thor Heyerdahl's crew and was swept along the Humboldt Current in the balsa raft Kon-Tiki. I read about the special powers of yoga masters and deep meditation, and hopped on a photon with none other than Albert Einstein, and together we screamed across the universe at the speed of light. I am certain there has never been a Latin student who felt the sheer exuberance I experienced in that second section of Latin 101. Mrs. Whiteman had inadvertently opened a portal to unknown and abstract realms into which I eagerly entered. And there I continue to dwell today, even while tending to the concerns of everyday living, making the mundane mystical.

As I grew over the years, my love of the abstract found many and varied practical applications. I became interested in the mental side of martial arts, read a book, and learned how to hypnotize my friends, discovered how to reduce pain and increase strength through meditation techniques, and, as a chiropractor, studied half-a-hundred healing procedures, from manipulating a joint to multiplying bioenergy. I fell in awe of Einstein's orientation of the universe and learned to appreciate the nonsensical reality of quantum physics. Those unusual, non-classical snippets of ingenious lunacy began to work their way into my mind, my heart, and even my perception of daily reality. And that brings us to the present, or almost.

Several years ago I had an epiphany. We all know that too much mental activity actually interferes with the success of activity. When the daily goings-on of talking, working, learning, and loving flow from a quieter state of mind, those activities become easier and yield far more fulfilling and successful results. This realization by itself is not new by any stretch of the imagination. After all it is the foundation for meditation, healing chronic diseases, the creative arts, and crafting the perfect jump shot. During my revelation I discovered that one can actually "do nothing" mentally, a kind of getting out of the way and letting Nature take its course, after which remarkable things begin to happen. I saw the entire universe as non-moving, frozen in time. I didn't know it at the time but later research revealed that this perception of non-movement had been established theoretically by Einstein and others. Just like the beginning, middle, and end of a movie are all contained within a single DVD, so the whole story of the universe is frozen beyond time. But we still haven't gotten to the exciting part.

I have always felt that there is nothing wrong with having your head in the clouds as long as you have your feet on the ground. What good is the perception of a timeless universe if it has no practical application? Now here is the exciting part! Along with the perception of an absolutely non-moving universe came the technique of non-doing: how to create fulfillment, fun, and success starting by doing nothing at all. It turns out that every one of us already has timelessness built into our genes. Timelessness is the touchstone for deepest success. Those people who give stillness a place of honor in their lives are themselves happier, more successful, compassionate, creative, and loving. There are more of these people around than you might imagine, and later in this book we will devote a whole chapter to their virtues so you can recognize those virtues when they appear in you. The point here is that because of a simple flash of insight I had in a moment of extraordinary lucidity, and we now have a practical process that balances our lives between inner stillness and its dynamic and vivacious application to outer life. The profundity of this technique might not immediately be appreciated until you realize that it unifies rather than polarizes.

Here's what I mean.

Every created thing is made of two parts: energy and form. The most basic form of energy is the wave. Waves combine to make subatomic particles which combine to make atoms, molecules, ending with the book you hold in your hand. This book has energy, doesn't it? You could use it to squash a mosquito or you could burn it to keep warm. (I hope that is the only reason you would have to burn this book.) Even thoughts and emotions have energy and form. They are just not as tangible as other objects. This book contains the energy of my thoughts and emotions, which when read stimulate similar thoughts and emotions in your mind. When you burn the book, heat and light are released. When you read the book, knowledge is released. All form has energy and all energy has form.

You have already identified a "field" of life that has neither energy nor form when you perceived pure awareness. That means that pure awareness is not created. Pure awareness is the progenitor of all created things whether they be tangible, ethereal, or otherwise. So if pure awareness has no form or energy what does that make it? We have said that it is nothing. That means that pure awareness contains "no thing" or no form. Pure awareness also contains no energy. Remember an object has form and energy. So a non-object has no form and no energy. The word we use for no form is nothing. The word we use for no energy is *stillness*.

When you talk about pure awareness you can say that it is complete nothing or you can say that it is absolute stillness. However, when perceiving pure awareness it is important to note that your mind considers nothing uninteresting, not worthy of its exalted attention. In a very abstract yet holistic way, stillness seems to draw your mind into it. That is why the EuStillness Technique works so quickly and completely to bring about all-inclusive life changes.

Simply put, we begin to see unity where diversity once reigned. And as we will soon discover, it is the ability to see unity, the coming together of two things to create greater harmony, that will save our collective bacon. So the EuStillness Technique offers us the perception of unity which automatically and instantly leads to greater success in life. We are not talking about the usual lifetime of work and study that has been subscribed to awareness of unity in the past. The "shift" is immediate, and then it's just a matter of letting the pieces fall into place. All things considered, this is pretty amazing.

Here's what I mean about the immediate influence of perception. When you hear screeching brakes and turn to see a dog being hit by a car, you immediately experience both physical and emotional changes, don't you? Physically you will have a quickening pulse, increased cardiac output, contraction of fight-or-flight musculature, hormonal shifts including a major squirt of adrenaline, dilated pupils, and much more. Emotionally you may experience fright, anxiety, confusion, anger, helplessness, compassion, etc. Now, consider watching a beautiful sunset. Your body becomes relaxed and your mind treasures an inner tranquility garnished with a dash of awe. The point is, all these changes take place automatically and instantly. You don't have to try to create them, do you? You don't need imagination, faith, or belief for perception to work. You don't even need to understand how it works. Your body and mind already know everything that needs to be known. They are etched into your genetic blueprint, the result of eons of evolutionary survival. Herein lies the genius of the EuStillness Technique which you will learn. Everything you need to experience what it means to be fully human is just waiting for you to take it for a test drive.

What is EuStillness and why is it beneficial? The initial stroke, that of going inward, is to first experience the nothing of pure awareness and its first glimmer of individuality in the mind, Eufeeling. Contained within Eufeeling is unending stillness. You will discover this endless stillness when you do the EuStillness Technique. The perception of this profound stillness we call EuStillness. (Also known as Pure Eufeeling.) EuStillness wakes up the finest level of our understanding mind, our intellect, the part of us that decides, among other things, what to do and when to do it, right from wrong and good from bad. This "waking up" of your intellect within EuStillness lets you see wholeness in the diversity of life. I know this may sound a little counterintuitive at this point, but when you perceive EuStillness, the stillness that is at the core of every created thing including stars, cars, and candy bars, you grasp wholly the unity of all life. EuStillness is the glue that holds your world together.

The final stroke of the EuStillness Technique is external. At this point we turn our gaze outward and inspect the phenomenal world we inhabit. Through the EuStillness Technique we observe the balancing and counterbalancing influence of EuStillness. We find and appreciate the common ground between opposites like pain and pleasure, man and woman, good and bad. Everything in your life will find its natural place. You will find your place in the great scheme of things and at last feel at home.

My goodness, I get goose bumps just thinking about it. I know this may sound incredibly abstract and currently beyond your reach, but please be assured it is not. I would not waste my time or yours if it were. Remember: "head in the clouds and feet on the ground". This is what I am talking about. You do not need to understand EuStillness to do the EuStillness Technique. You already have everything you need for that. I can guarantee that, and one more thing: Once EuStillness is lively in your life, all this will make perfect sense.

So how does the EuStillness Technique work? Well, not by conventional laws, that is for sure. When you think about it, a technique is how to *do* something, isn't it? Well, how can you do something to do nothing? Of course, that seems impossible. It seems to make sense that you cannot generate an activity of non-activity. This is the very reason many meditation and spiritual techniques take so long to yield results. They expect the student to create inner stillness or become an unmoving observer by doing something, like creating positive thoughts, concentrating on a word or idea, or bending and breathing in just the right way. This is the very opposite of their goal of inner peace or being the silent observer. Movement, mental or otherwise, does not lead to stillness. Stillness exists in spite of movement. Traditional "doing" techniques are successful only when the mind gets tired and momentarily gives up doing the prescribed technique. At the moment it gives up, the mind stops. It is when the mind stops working that it discovers stillness waiting with open arms. The EuStillness Technique skips the getting tired part and goes right to stillness.

The EuStillness Technique is a kind of shift in perception from doing to being that is so natural that relaxation and inner peace are the immediate result, followed quickly by measurable levels of healing and, later, even more profound results. I did not set out to develop a simple, scientific technique. It just appeared one day in seed form; all I had to do was let it germinate and grow.

OK, so what this means in plain language is I stumbled upon a way to *do* nothing. You heard me right: do nothing. It gets better. It turns out that doing nothing is necessary if anything is to get done. I know it sounds crazy, but it's true. In fact, it has always been true. If we want to do anything we must always start by going in the opposite direction first. Sounds bizarre? Think about it.

If you want to get out of that chair you are sitting in then what is the first thing you must do? That's right! You must first push *down* with your feet and hands if you want to stand *up*. If you then choose to walk to your fridge for a cold drink, you must first push your foot in the opposite direction from the fridge so that you will move forward toward that beer in the icebox. If you want to drive a nail you begin by moving the hammer in the opposite direction. If you want to build a skyscraper you start by digging a hole.

Now here comes the do-nothing part. When you stop going in the opposite direction and just before you go forward you are completely at rest, aren't you? When your foot is done pushing backward and just before it swings forward, it is at rest. When you raise the hammer back it stops just before you swing it forward. You see, doing nothing is built into every activity.

Even the simplest form of activity in creation, the sine wave, exhibits this do-nothing-to-do-something principle. The sine wave goes up, then down, then up, then down, and that's all it does for its whole life. But it's not just work, work, work, for the lowly sine wave. After each up and after each down he gets to take a short rest, something like a coffee break. It appears that the universe is a benevolent employer, building rest, the art of doing nothing, into every activity even at the most basic level of creation.

Now would be a good time to take a closer look at this fascinating principle. Let's take the example of shooting an arrow at a target. This is a great analogy for uncovering the principles of dynamic action and success, the very founding principles at work in the EuStillness Technique.

Now let's say that you want to shoot an arrow at a target. What is the first thing you must do? You must first draw the arrow in the opposite direction from the target. Isn't that right? Once you have drawn the arrow back fully and just before you release it the arrow is at rest, isn't it? It is in a different state of rest than if the arrow were just lying on the ground. The fully drawn arrow displays a dynamic rest. It is not moving but has the full potential to do so as soon as you release it.

What do you do next? You aim at the target, don't you? Now, once you have fully drawn the arrow and aimed it at the target, what must you do to get the arrow into the target? That's right ... Nothing! Before you release the arrow your muscles are tense holding the arrow in place. All you have to do is *stop doing.* In this case, you let your muscles relax and instantly the arrow takes flight. If your aim is true you will score a bull's-eye. This is exactly how the EuStillness Technique works.

The arrow represents the ability of your mind to create successful action, to get what you want. When you nock the arrow but have not yet pulled it back, the arrow is just sitting there. If you let go of the arrow at this point it just falls to the ground. This represents the inactivity of your mind during deep sleep. If you were to pull the arrow back several inches, this would represent the potential of your mind during everyday common consciousness. Pulling the arrow back just a few inches and releasing it propels the arrow forward but nowhere near its full potential. It may take several attempts to hit the target, if at all. Taking a full draw on the arrow and then releasing it toward the target represents acting from our full potential. A full draw is like taking your awareness through common consciousness all the way to pure awareness and Eufeeling. Now here is the beautiful thing about the EuStillness Technique. After you have fully drawn the arrow and it is in the state of dynamic rest, the next thing you do is point the arrow at the target. With the arrow fully drawn and pointing at the target, you stop doing and instantly the arrow flies true and strikes the center ring. When you do the EuStillness Technique you draw the mind fully to pure awareness, become aware of EuStillness, and then Eufeeling. Becoming aware of EuStillness sets your mind at dynamic stillness ready for fullness of action. Becoming aware of Eufeeling is like pointing the arrow at the target, and with the full potential of EuStillness behind it, you hit the target. Once aware of EuStillness, mentally you do nothing while Eufeeling moves you, your body and mind, toward hitting your target, be it personal, financial, educational, or spiritual.

That's it! As you can see, there's nothing to it. In almost everything we do in life we put emphasis on the doing and ignore the not-doing. Doing and doing, then doing some more, is tiring. Everything is thrown out of balance when we don't factor in silent, harmonizing stillness. How do we "factor in" dynamic stillness? Well, I think it is time you learned the EuStillness Technique, don't you?

Main Points – Chapter 3

- Einstein and others have theoretically established a non-moving universe.

- Timelessness (non-movement) is the touchstone for deepest success.

- Every created thing is made of two parts, energy and form.

- Pure awareness is "nothing", absolute stillness.

- A perception instantly affects both body and mind.

- The perception of nothing (stillness) is necessary for dynamic activity.

- The perception of EuStillness is awareness of pure awareness while thinking and doing.

CHAPTER 4

DISCOVERING THE MUSIC INSIDE US:

How to Find Eufeeling

*"Most of us go to our graves
with our music still inside us."*

~ OLIVER WENDELL HOLMES

Oliver Wendell Holmes, in the quote above, is telling us that we are missing something. Or more rightly,
we are ignoring something so vital that without it life
loses its music, the very thing that gives it substance. I am
reminded of the shadow world of Plato's cave where the
cave-dwellers believed the totality of life to be flickering
shadows thrown on the cave walls by firelight. There they
sat, observing and debating the reality of their shadow existence. All they had to do to experience life in all its glory,
the pungent smell of earth, the gentle sighing of the wind,
the vibrant blues and reds and yellows of a meadow in full

bloom, was simply to turn around and look out the mouth of their cave. At that very moment they added their music to the symphony that is life.

You are a unique instrument in the symphony of life. (I know, I know, pretty corny but it makes the point.) You must play the music you are. A drum cannot play violin music. To play the music you are, you must first find the music you are. Your inner music, the harmony that sings in symphony with all creation, is your distinctive display of Eufeeling. Aware of Eufeeling, you cannot go to your grave with your music still inside. You step out of the shadows into the full light of day. Like a bird cannot stop itself from sharing its song with the world, once you are aware of Eufeeling the song that you are will burst forth upon this world with joyous thunder.

To do the EuStillness Technique you must first become aware of Eufeeling. To become aware of Eufeeling you must first become aware of pure awareness. You became aware of pure awareness when you watched the screen of your mind in The Nothing Technique. Congratulations, you are already one-third of the way there. Becoming aware of Eufeeling is just as simple and just as easy. So, unless you have a heavy date or are burning something in the oven for dinner I think it's time I introduced you to that most intimate part of you, the first glimmer of individuality that makes you, you ... Eufeeling. We'll begin by reviewing The Nothing Technique and pick it up from there.

As before, you can read the instructions all the way through a couple of times and then follow them by memory. You can read the instructions into a recorder, pausing 4 to 5 seconds after each sentence, or you can have someone read them to you. Or you can get the audio download of me guiding you through the *Eufeeling Technique* via the website at: www.KinslowSystem.com/learn.html.

OK, let's begin ...

The Eufeeling Technique

Close your eyes and let your mind wander wherever it wants to go. Now become aware of what you are thinking. The content is not important, just know that thoughts are there. Easily watch your thoughts as if you were watching a movie. Just let your thoughts flow across the screen of your mind. You are looking at your thoughts ... Now easily look past the thoughts and notice that there is nothing there. Continue to be aware of nothing as long as is comfortable. When thoughts begin again, watch them briefly and then again look beyond them, or between them, at nothing. Do this for 2 to 3 minutes.

Now become aware of how you feel. You will have some sense of well-being, some good feeling. It might be a sense of lightness or expansion, a feeling of silence or peace. You may even feel joy or love or bliss. It does not matter what good feeling you have, just become aware of it. This good feeling, this peace or lightness, joy or fullness, is your Eufeeling. Now continue to watch your Eufeeling with easy attention.

Easily watch your Eufeeling to see what it will do. It will change in some way; all you need to do is be aware of how it changes. Your Eufeeling can become very quiet or very strong. It can change into another Eufeeling. For instance, a feeling of lightness could transform into bliss or unboundedness. One Eufeeling is no better than another. You may also notice that your Eufeeling disappears altogether leaving only pure awareness. Pure awareness is not a goal. It is simply another experience that you can have while you are observing Eufeeling. No matter how it changes, your intent is to simply watch Eufeeling without interfering.

You will also observe thoughts coming and going. Thoughts will always come and go and should never be opposed. Thoughts, noises, bodily sensations, etc., are all OK. You should not resent them. Whenever you become aware that you are having a thought or sensation, here's what you do: easily let your awareness go back to your Eufeeling.

Now, continue this process of observing Eufeeling, watching it change, and when it is no longer there letting your awareness gently return to Eufeeling. Do this quietly for 3 to 5 minutes and then allow your eyes to slowly open and continue reading.

Welcome back. Now that your eyes are opened, how are you feeling? Do you feel some relaxation in your body? What are you feeling in your mind? Do you feel some inner sense of well-being? Maybe you feel silence or peace or a sense of relief, joy, bliss, compassion, or lightness. Take a moment and become aware of that good feeling. That is your Eufeeling. Guess what? Your eyes are open and you are aware of Eufeeling! Isn't that remarkable? You had to close your eyes to find Eufeeling, but now you have found it with your eyes wide open. Eufeeling is everywhere all the time. When you become aware of Eufeeling, eyes open or closed, you are poised to realize your full potential. You have fully drawn your arrow back and are ready to be point it at the target.

Do you see how simple this is? Regardless of what appears on the screen of your mind, your position is always the same. You are the observer, nothing more. *Never interfere or try to control either your thoughts or your Eufeeling.* Believe me – everything will be taken care of for you. Did you have to work at becoming relaxed or feeling peaceful? No, it's all automatic. It's all taken care of for you through the wisdom of your Eufeeling once you become aware of it. Don't complicate it or you will stop the process in its tracks and, slowly, but most assuredly, return to common everyday consciousness.

Remember that your Eufeeling is unbounded, so it's always there. You've just been ignoring it most of your life. And you will ignore it again unless you make a conscious effort not to. With just a moment's reflection you can become aware of Eufeeling. Do it now. Pause for just a second or two ... Are you aware of Eufeeling, aware of some sense of well-being, some good feeling? Excellent, that is all you need, simple awareness of Eufeeling.

Now look at an object in front of you. While you observe that object, become aware of Eufeeling. Look at another object and become aware of Eufeeling. Now slowly get to your feet and become aware of Eufeeling. Move around the room involving all of your senses. Listen to the noises in the room and become aware of Eufeeling. Feel your clothes moving against your skin as you walk and become aware of Eufeeling. Smell the air with Eufeeling. Eat something and pay attention to the multitude of tastes that explode in your mouth while aware of Eufeeling.

Have you noticed that while you are aware of Eufeeling you are not worried about paying the bills, that problem at work, or smoothing ruffled feathers in your relationship? Again become aware of Eufeeling for a few seconds. Now notice that you feel whole, somehow complete. You really need for nothing. You see, your life is already mending itself. And how is it doing it? Your healing is taking place effortlessly, naturally, and with the greatest ease. If you were to learn nothing else but how to become aware of Eufeeling, in time you would blossom fully and beautifully as each of us should.

If you were not immediately aware of Eufeeling when you opened your eyes, again close your eyes and repeat the Eufeeling Technique. In a very short time, in a matter of days, you will recognize Eufeeling anytime, anywhere. Until you learn the EuStillness Technique I recommend that you do the Eufeeling Technique for 4 to 5 minutes, three times a day. The best times are first thing in the morning, last thing at night, and somewhere in the middle of your day, say at lunchtime or when you get home from work. Also, whenever you think about it, pause momentarily and become aware of your Eufeeling. You might be driving, talking, working, cooking, etc. Pause long enough (1 to 2 seconds, longer if you like) to become aware of Eufeeling. Then just easily let it go.

You are laying the foundation for a life that is beyond imagination. Somewhere in the not-too-distant future you will all of a sudden realize that your life has become, without effort, fuller, more meaningful, and more fun. Right now you are learning a new skill. You are culturing your mind to function on a quieter, more organized yet more dynamic level. Approach your new skills and your new world with a sense of playfulness and discovery. And remember, if it isn't easy and it isn't fun, then you have slipped back into common consciousness. The remedy is easy. Are you aware of Eufeeling ...

In a Nutshell:
The Eufeeling Technique

- Sit comfortably with your eyes closed, and let your mind wander wherever it wants to go.

- Easily watch your thoughts like watching a movie.

- Now look beyond or between your thoughts and become aware of nothing.

- When thoughts return, again easily look beyond thoughts to find nothing (1 to 3 minutes).

- Now become aware of the good feeling, your Eufeeling – silence, peace, joy, lightness, etc.

- Observe your Eufeeling with clear but simple innocence. It will get stronger or change into another Eufeeling, or new thoughts will come.

- Whatever happens, just watch without interfering (3 to 4 minutes).

- When you open your eyes, move around the room and use all your senses to explore your environment while becoming aware of Eufeeling.

- When you realize that your Eufeeling has slipped away, just look to find that sense of well-being, that good feeling. Close your eyes if necessary. Observe Eufeeling for a while, and then continue to explore other objects.

Main Points – Chapter 4

- To become aware of Eufeeling you must first be aware of pure awareness.

- Eufeeling is unbounded. It's always there whether you are aware of it or not.

- While aware of Eufeeling, you need for nothing.

- Do the Eufeeling Technique for 4 to 5 minutes, three times a day.

- In a very short time, in a matter of days, you will recognize Eufeeling anytime, anywhere.

CHAPTER 5

HOW TO DO THE EUSTILLNESS TECHNIQUE

"Simplicity is the ultimate sophistication."

~LEONARDO DA VINCI

Now for the really good stuff! In a few moments you will learn the EuStillness Technique. The genius of this procedure is that it engenders, almost without effort, EuStillness, a perception so profound and pervasive that from your very first contact EuStillness begins to rearrange and stabilize the foundation stones upon which the rest of your life will be lived. This is not something apart from you or being done to you. The perception of EuStillness is the perception of you in complete harmony. Stresses and physical degradation, misconceptions and mistreatment, missed opportunities, and missed loved ones weaken and destabilize your mind and body. Soon, you begin to believe the world is your adversary and you brace yourself against the next blow. EuStillness is a healing salve for every injury you have endured.

You remember earlier when we discussed how your body and mind have immediate reactions to your perceptions? The perception of EuStillness is the perception of complete harmony, and that perfection is reflected instantly in both your body and your mind. It is not imaginary. It is very, very real and you will know it right away. It is only that this most exquisite perception has been hidden from you under layers and layers of misdirection and mental detritus built up over the years. A single perception of EuStillness can wash away the weariness and worry of a lifetime. Certainly regular practice will net you profound results in a way that you will never expect but will come to love.

That is the way EuStillness works. It fixes things you don't even know need fixing. It's kind of like having a chauffeur who is also a car mechanic. You let the chauffeur drive you around town and if anything breaks down he gets out and fixes it. OK, OK, I know that's not the best analogy I've come up with, but I think you get what I'm driving at. (Pun intended – no groaning or I will send you back to Chapter 1 to start all over again.) That's better.

Now, before you learn the EuStillness Technique you must feel at home with Eufeeling. After all, you won't be able to experience EuStillness if you first don't know Eufeeling. Eufeeling is everywhere all the time, so you should be able to become aware of it just about anywhere, anytime. That means you just have the thought, "Is Eufeeling there?" and your awareness goes effortlessly to it. It's just like your refrigerator motor. When it is running you don't pay attention to it. You don't hear it at all. But then if you say, "Is my refrigerator motor running?" your awareness effortlessly goes to the refrigerator motor and you hear that it is running. In the beginning you may have to close your eyes to become aware of Eufeeling, but after doing the Eufeeling Technique for a short while you will begin to notice that Eufeeling is with you anytime you think of it, even with your eyes open.

So if you don't feel completely at home with Eufeeling, then go back to the previous chapter and perform the Eufeeling Technique until you are easy with Eufeeling. You may have to do the Eufeeling Technique for several days or longer, but don't be in a hurry. The Eufeeling Technique is fun, and a few extra days of fun never hurt anybody. As Maharishi, an old teacher of mine used to say, "Well begun is half done."

Tada! You and your Eufeeling are old buddies and now it's time for you to learn the EuStillness Technique. Find a comfortable seat in a quiet place where you will not be disturbed for 20 minutes or so. You can read through the instructions a couple of times and then perform the EuStillness Technique from memory. I do not recommend this unless it is the only choice you have, because learning of the EuStillness Technique is quite long to trust to memory. If at all possible, read the instructions into a recorder and play them back, or have someone read them to you, pausing for 4 to 5 seconds after each sentence (unless otherwise noted). The first two parts of this teaching will be familiar to you. They will prepare you for the actual perception of EuStillness. All right, here we go ...

The EuStillness Technique

Sit comfortably and close your eyes. Let your mind wander wherever it wants to go. Become aware of what you are thinking. Just watch your thoughts as they flow across the screen of your mind. The content of your thoughts is not important. Just become aware that you are having thoughts. Notice that beyond your thoughts is space containing nothing. Now let your awareness go to the space beyond your thoughts.

As you are aware of the space sometimes thoughts will return. When you realize your awareness is on your thoughts then just shift your awareness back to the space. Don't resent the thoughts or try to keep your awareness in the space. This is not necessary. Only do this: When you realize your awareness is on thoughts, let it shift easily and effortlessly to the space beyond or between thought. Do this for 2 to 3 minutes ...

Now become aware of how you feel. You will have some sense of well-being, some good feeling. It might be a sense of lightness or expansion, a feeling of silence or peace. You may even feel joy or love or bliss. Sometimes only pure awareness is there without a feeling attached to it. You may say, "I am feeling nothing." This is just fine. Pure awareness of nothing is your Eufeeling. It does not matter what Eufeeling you have, just become easily aware of it. This good feeling, this peace or lightness, joy or fullness, or even the perception of nothing, is your Eufeeling.

Be attentive to your Eufeeling. It will change. Watch your Eufeeling to see how it will change. Eufeeling can get stronger or very quiet; it can change into another Eufeeling; it can disappear altogether so that you are aware of pure awareness, or thoughts may take its place. When you realize thoughts are there, then just allow your awareness to gently return to Eufeeling. Continue to watch your Eufeeling in this easy way for 1 to 3 minutes ...

Now become aware of Eufeeling however you are perceiving it: silence, peace, joy, bliss, lightness, unboundedness, compassion, awe, nothing, etc. Be very attentive to your Eufeeling. Watch it with a clear, easy wakefulness like a cat watching a mouse-hole. Look into Eufeeling as if it were a mouse-hole to *see what is inside. As you look attentively into Eufeeling it will begin to dissolve or dissipate like a gentle mist in bright sunlight. Look into Eufeeling as it dissolves to see what is there. When Eufeeling has dissolved there is only stillness. Become aware of the stillness.*

Stillness will eventually be replaced with thoughts. This is just fine. When thoughts return just easily allow your awareness to return to stillness. If stillness is not readily available, become aware of Eufeeling, then look into Eufeeling to find stillness waiting for you there. You can even look into thought. When you observe thought closely it too will dissolve into stillness. Continue to be aware of stillness for 1 to 3 minutes ...

Now become easily and clearly aware of stillness. Watch it like a cat watching a mouse-hole. Look into stillness as if it were a mouse-hole to see what is inside. When you attentively look into stillness you find greater stillness. Look clearly into the greater stillness to find greater stillness yet. Continue to easily yet attentively look into greater and greater stillness. If your awareness shifts to thoughts or Eufeeling, return again to stillness and greater stillness. Do this for 1 to 2 minutes ...

Become easily and attentively aware of stillness. Become aware of your whole body. Now become aware of stillness in your whole body. Become aware of your head and stillness. Become aware of your chest and stillness. Become aware of your arms and legs and stillness. Continue to visit localized areas of your body and become aware of the stillness therein. Do this for 1 minute ...

Now, again become aware of stillness in your mind. Look into that stillness to find greater stillness. Now take about 10 or 15 seconds and then slowly open your eyes. With eyes open become aware of your whole body and stillness. Look at an object in front of you and become aware of stillness. Find another object and stillness. Become aware of the space filling the room and stillness. Become aware of the space and all the objects and stillness.

Get easily to your feet and become aware of stillness. Explore your environment using all your senses. Touch a chair or the wall and become aware of stillness. Smell the air and stillness. Look at something colorful and stillness, something drab and stillness. Taste something and become aware of stillness. Now hold your hand out, palm facing you. Become aware of how your hand feels at the same time you are aware of stillness. Become aware of the space between your hand and your eyes and the stillness that is in that space. Become aware of the space between you and your hand, to the sides of your hand and behind your hand, and then become aware of the stillness in that space and your hand all at the same time. Become aware that you are standing in the room surrounded by the walls and the space within, and become aware of stillness in all of it. In your mind's eye see the Earth floating in the blackness of space and become aware of stillness in the Earth and space. See all of creation, every created thing contained within a single glistening cosmic egg floating in the unbounded vastness of space and become aware of stillness within every created thing and within the unbounded space beyond.

Return to your seat and sit quietly in stillness with your eyes closed for 1 minute ... Again let your awareness go to stillness. Look attentively into that stillness to find greater and even greater stillness. This absolute stillness that you are aware of is called EuStillness. Now aware of EuStillness, look for some reflection of Eufeeling. It will be there. Some tender impulse of joy or delight or compassion, bliss, peace, or love, some gentle good feeling. Like a leaf on a quiet pond, your Eufeeling gently rocks on the surface of EuStillness creating wavelets of Itself, wavelets of euphoria or joy or kindness or harmony that expand outward into your mind, your body, the room, the earth, and all creation. Sit easily aware of this gentle, all-pervading impulse of completeness for as little or as long as you like ...

Now let your mind wander wherever it wants to go. Take 20 or 30 seconds, or longer if you like, then slowly open your eyes. Pay attention to how you feel in both body and mind. How do you feel differently? Easily look around you. How has your perception changed? How does that make you feel? Finally, become aware of EuStillness and then find your Eufeeling in that stillness ... And enjoy.

Congratulations! You are now a EuStillness perceiver, which puts you in the one-half percentile of humans inhabiting this magnificent spaceship we call Earth. Welcome aboard. I recommend that you substitute the EuStillness Technique for the Eufeeling Technique that you have been doing. (See Chapter 15, On Becoming Fully Human: 90 Days of EuStillness.)

Start with 10 minutes or more first thing in the morning, last thing at night, and somewhere in the middle of your day. Don't worry, the silent time spent in EuStillness will be more than compensated for by your increased energy and productivity afterwards. Every time you think of it, become aware of EuStillness. You can become aware of EuStillness in your mind, your whole body or some part of it, your whole environment or some part of it, like a book or a tree. You only have to become aware of EuStillness for 2 to 3 seconds or so, but you can do it longer if you choose. The object is to become aware of EuStillness in as many different ways and as often as you think about it. In the beginning you may have to remind yourself, but it will be well worth the little bit of effort you may have to apply to remembering. Of course, there is no effort involved in the actual awareness of EuStillness.

You cannot force the perception of EuStillness. That would be trying – that is, creating an effort to do nothing. Remember the bow and arrow analogy? Once the arrow is drawn and aimed, doing anything more only veers the arrow off its mark. Trying is doing something; EuStillness is being nothing. However, after you are aware of EuStillness you can do things, all the things that you would normally do without EuStillness. Only now, the doing you do will be more fun, more fulfilling, and far more successful.

You may well be thinking that, yes, EuStillness is pretty remarkable. When I perceive it I feel stable and full like I am at the same time a part of Nature and the whole of it. My body is deeply relaxed and my mind deep at peace. There is no doubt about it: EuStillness is a profound perception – but what now?

What now indeed. Over their lives many people have felt isolated. Maybe you are one of them. These people feel out of step with the people and events going on around them. Aside from infrequent periods in their life where they may have felt temporarily comfortable with the status quo, they mostly feel like they don't quite fit into this world. They feel like square pegs being forced into round holes. These people have to give in and give up some part of themselves in order to fit into society. They must conform in a way that is unnatural for them.

These sequestered souls – and I firmly believe that I am talking about the majority of humanity – even feel estranged to themselves. They are frustrated that communication with their inner self, which should be effortless and nurturing, is disjointed and deeply disappointing. They are alienated from their own inner workings.

When you become aware of EuStillness you break through the illusion of separateness. When you perceive the stillness that permeates and surrounds all life, you begin to appreciate that all this comes from the same source. This is not a fanciful philosophy or intricate belief system but an actual realization that we truly are, in essence, all one. As you will realize for yourself, opening your awareness to the perception of EuStillness fosters a deep sense of connectedness within you and around you. You begin to realize with great affinity that where you are is exactly where you should be, and it feels great.

Some have called EuStillness the ultimate perception of unity binding all differences within its oneness. Aware of EuStillness you have fully drawn the arrow and, left to your own devices over time, would strike the center ring of your worldly targets with greater accuracy and frequency. In other words, just by the virtue of being aware of EuStillness you will obtain what you need from life by doing less work, or doing nothing, and achieving more and more success. That's if you just walk away right now and did nothing more than become aware of EuStillness on a daily basis. But why would you do that? You haven't finished this book. I have a lot more in store for you, and now that you have discovered EuStillness for yourself I am going to show you how to "use" it to pick more meaningful targets and hit the bull's-eye more often and have far more fun doing it.

How does healing strike your fancy? Would you like to be able to stimulate the healing response for all kinds of physical calamities including everything from sprains and arthritis, indigestion and hypertension, and even serious and chronic conditions like chronic fatigue, diabetes, and even cancer? You can deeply and positively influence any physical distress in you, in others, and even in your pets. What's more, your healing influence begins the very moment you become aware of EuStillness.

But there is more. What you can do with physical pain and discomfort you can also apply to emotional discord. Or, how about relationships? Is everything going perfectly with yours? To understand how to apply EuStillness in re-lationships we will call on the theory of transformation and help you figure out where you are, where you need to go, and how to get there. I will even teach you how to make a decision in EuStillness. What about your spiritual life? You may not have realized it yet, but awareness of EuStillness cloaks you in the finest of spiritual garments spun from threads of universal love. Before you leave, we will discuss what universal love is, and then together – for that is the only way unbounded love works – we will open our awareness and allow universal love to wash over us.

In a Nutshell:
The EuStillness Technique

- Do the Nothing Technique (1 minute).

- Do the Eufeeling Technique (1 to 3 minutes).

- Watch your Eufeeling with clear, easy wakefulness.

- Look into your Eufeeling as it dissolves into absolute stillness (EuStillness).

- Become aware of EuStillness (1 to 3 minutes).

- When thoughts come – easily become aware of EuStillness.

- Look into EuStillness to find greater stillness (1 to 2 minutes).

- Become aware of your whole body/parts of your body and EuStillness (1 minute).

- Return to EuStillness close your eyes and become aware of objects/space and EuStillness.

- Walk around using your senses with awareness of EuStillness.

- Become aware of all creation and beyond and EuStillness.

- Sit down with eyes closed in EuStillness (1 minute).

- Find your Eufeeling floating in EuStillness.

- Open eyes slowly/how do you feel/how has your perception changed?

- Become aware of EuStillness – find your Eufeeling – enjoy!

Main Points – Chapter 5

- The perception of EuStillness is the perception of you in complete harmony.

- The most efficient way to find EuStillness is through Eufeeling.

- To establish EuStillness, become aware of it in as many different ways as you can.

- You cannot force the perception of EuStillness.

- When you become aware of EuStillness, you break through the illusion of separateness.

- Some have called EuStillness the ultimate perception of unity binding all differences within its oneness.

CHAPTER 6

THE STOP-HAND
TECHNIQUE

*"Once you eliminate the impossible, whatever remains,
no matter how improbable, must be the truth."*
~ SIR ARTHUR CONAN DOYLE, THE SIGN OF FOUR

You are learning a new skill. Yes, the EuStillness Technique is virtually an effortless perception that broadens and stabilizes your view of the world. It is a natural technique – that is, you were born with everything you need to do it. But just as you were born with everything you need to have a conversation with your next-door neighbor, you still needed to learn how to talk, right? The good news is learning to apply EuStillness to your life is way, way easier than learning to talk – and a whole lot more fun.

At this point in your life when you speak to someone you don't even think about forming syllables and sounds with your teeth, tongue, and lips. You just have a thought and speech flutters fluently from your mouth like rose petals on coronation day at a florist's convention. Well, you know what I mean. Speech is natural but it took some practice to learn, and because you did so you now have one of the most powerful tools on Earth. EuStillness is natural but it will also take some practice for you to learn. When you do you will have the most powerful perception open to human awareness. With that in mind I would like to teach you the Stop-Hand Technique. Stop-Hand will provide you the basics for EuStillness awareness.

The Stop-Hand Technique

Before starting, become aware of EuStillness for a few seconds (or longer if you like). Open your hand in front of you with your elbow slightly bent and your palm facing outward. Think of a police officer making the "stop" gesture when directing traffic. Look at everything in front of your hand. For instance, if you are indoors you might see furniture, books, knickknacks, pictures, etc. Casually take in the scene in front of your open hand. Now close your eyes and the objects will remain in your mind for a little while. Become aware of EuStillness. Become easily and clearly aware of that complete stillness. EuStillness will quickly become more dominant in your awareness than the objects in your mind. The mental picture you have of those objects in the room will diminish as EuStillness becomes more dominant. Now become aware of both EuStillness and the objects in the room. You might notice that the objects themselves are made of EuStillness. It is as if stillness is their very essence, which of course it is.

Now open your eyes and become aware of EuStillness. Hold your hand out again and become aware of the room objects in front of your hand. Become aware of this stillness within the objects themselves. Just like in your mind, the real objects are also made of EuStillness. Continue to observe the EuStillness within the objects with your awareness more on this stillness.

Soon EuStillness will become more dominant in your awareness and the objects less dominant. They seem to fade a little as the stillness becomes stronger. This perception may not occur right away, but as you practice the Stop-Hand Technique with your eyes open you will recognize EuStillness around you more and more. We are not quite done.

At present, you have your eyes open and your hand extended while you are aware of EuStillness in the objects in the room. Now become aware of EuStillness within your whole body. Along with this shift of perception you might also notice some pleasant sensations (Eufeeling) throughout your body. Enjoy those pleasant sensations but allow your awareness to be with EuStillness in your body.

Now become aware of EuStillness in your body and the objects in the room both at the same time. Again, allow your awareness to fall clearly and easily on Eufeeling until it becomes more dominant than your body or the objects in the room.

Next, become aware of your body, the objects in the room, and the space between your body and the objects. Become aware of EuStillness within that space. Again, become gently but attentively aware of Eufeeling in your body, the objects, and the space between. Basically, you are first becoming aware of EuStillness and then Eufeeling.

Finally, become aware of EuStillness within you, in front of you, and all around you. Now let your mind travel outward into space encompassing the Earth, our galaxy, and all of creation. Observe that all is supported by and interpenetrated by EuStillness. Now let your mind go to smaller and smaller levels of existence. See that molecules are made of atoms, and atoms of subatomic particles, and subatomic particles of waves. Observe that all microscopic existence is also supported by and interpenetrated by EuStillness.

Find yourself back in your room where EuStillness is in you and all around you. Become clearly aware of that stillness. Now become aware of your Eufeeling shining through the stillness. It can be peace, joy, love, delight, ecstasy, awe, or any of the other reflections of Eufeeling. Let your awareness be comfortably with Eufeeling and enjoy ...

The Stop-Hand Technique is designed to make you conscious of the fact that EuStillness is not only everywhere all the time, but is actually the essence of every object, thought, and emotion. It also lets you see how Eufeeling shines through EuStillness. The value of this perception is beyond compare. It catapults us beyond our limited, day-to-day existence, opening our awareness to possibilities yet unthought-of.

For instance, EuStillness gives us direct perception of the sameness of all things. You have probably heard that we are all one. What does that mean? Look at another human being. No two look the same, nor do they think the same thoughts. Where is the oneness? "We are all one" is a beautiful philosophy, but without direct experience of that oneness it remains a fanciful philosophy with little practical application. Not so anymore. Perception of EuStillness gives us not only direct experience of the sameness between two people but between everything created including trees, bees, and dimpled knees, to name a few.

You may very well ask, "What is the value of seeing the sameness of everything?" You are a very discerning reader and I applaud you for asking that question. When you perceive what is the same between you and another person, or thing, you lose your fear of that person or thing. Isn't that true? We endeavor to gather around us those things that are like us. We feel more comfortable, more secure, don't we? Now think back to when your mind is fully engaged in EuStillness. Didn't you feel whole and at home? Was there any room for fear or anger? It is impossible to feel jealousy or revenge when you are aware of EuStillness.

I have only touched on one of the benefits of EuStillness awareness, but what a whopper! What would the peoples of the world give for freedom from fear? How ironic that fearless living already abides within them. Imagine what would happen if the world population were to become aware of EuStillness for one day. Then imagine their elation when they found out that fear-free living is open to and easily attainable for each and every one of them, not 20 years down the road but immediately. My goodness, what goodness we would harvest.

Once you get the hang of the Stop-Hand Technique you will be able to do it with your eyes open just about anywhere you happen to be. I've done it at the barbershop, at the gym, and even while sneaking an extra scoop of Chunky Monkey ice cream from the freezer, as well as in many other varied and interesting times and places. Remember to have fun. Initially you will probably want to start practicing Stop-Hand sitting in a quiet place where you can close your eyes. I recommend that you do the Stop-Hand Technique several times a day. Actually, when you're just starting out you can add it to the end of your EuStillness Technique. As you become more adept at perceiving EuStillness with your eyes open, you can do abbreviated sessions. With practice you will be able to instantly perceive EuStillness in everything, all around you. Then, just pick up your Eufeeling and off you go. Total time elapsed: 3 seconds. Experiment, do it often, and have fun. It can't be done any other way.

In a Nutshell:
The Stop-Hand Technique

- Become aware of EuStillness.

- Hold out "stop" hand.

- Become aware of objects in front of your hand.

- Close your eyes and become aware of objects in your mind.

- Become aware of EuStillness until more dominant than objects.

- Become aware of both EuStillness and objects.

- Open your eyes and become aware of EuStillness.

- Become aware of objects in front of your hand.

- Become aware of EuStillness until stronger than the objects.

- Become aware of EuStillness in your whole body.

- Become aware of EuStillness in your body and objects until stronger.

- Become aware of EuStillness in body, objects, and the space between until stronger.

- Become aware of EuStillness within you and all around you.

- Become aware of EuStillness on all levels of creation.

- Become aware of your Eufeeling in EuStillness.

Main Points – Chapter 6

- EuStillness is natural but it will also take some practice for you to learn.

- The Stop-Hand Technique will provide you with the basics for EuStillness awareness.

- Stop-Hand is designed to make you conscious of the fact that EuStillness is the essence of every object, thought, and emotion, everywhere, all the time.

- It is impossible to feel fear, jealousy, or revenge when you are aware of EuStillness.

- With practice you will be able to instantly perceive EuStillness in everything, all around you.

CHAPTER 7

HEALING WITH EUSTILLNESS

"I have often regretted my speech, never my silence."
~XENOCRATES (396–314 BC)

Imagine that you are playing tennis with a friend. She goes to the forecourt to field your drop shot and turns her ankle. She lets out a shriek of agony and then gives you a furious look for playing that last shot. Within minutes her ankle is swollen and purple and throbbing with pain. You gently encircle her ankle with your hands and become aware of EuStillness. Within minutes the swelling and bruising disappear and the pain is but a memory. Sounds like something you would like to be able to do? You already can!

Once you understand the principles of healing you will wonder why all of us aren't doing it all of the time. So let's take a few lines to look at how healing takes place, and then we'll learn how to create a healing event for both physical and emotional discord.

No matter what ails you, physical, chemical, or emotional, healing cannot take place without rest. What does rest mean in the healing sense? It means reducing activity sufficiently enough so that reorganization in the injured area can take place. After all, you can't perform heart surgery if the patient is running around the table.

We can best understand this principle, although I think it's pretty obvious, by revisiting your friend with the sprained ankle above. If she were to continue to play tennis, do you think her injury would repair itself? Of course it wouldn't. Continual activity at the site of injury would hinder or render useless all those natural processes that must work in symphony with each other for healing to be realized.

Here's a good way to look at it. Healing comes from rest. Rest is less activity. Less activity is more harmony. No activity is perfect harmony. EuStillness, absolute stillness, is perfect harmony. It's just one more step for us to say that EuStillness creates the perfect environment for healing to take place.

The really neat thing is that when you perceive EuStillness you instantly create a healing environment within and around. You don't have to do anything else. You don't have to know how to do surgery, dispense medication, massage a rhomboid muscle, insert an acupuncture needle, or work with angels or healing energies. All that comes after you becomes aware of EuStillness. If you are a surgeon and become aware of EuStillness, you are now the best surgeon you can be for both yourself and your patient.

Healing takes in a lot of territory and there are all levels and kinds of healing. In fact, there are literally hundreds of thousands of healing techniques, all with their own philosophy and mode of application. Some are quite simple and others most bizarre, but we don't have to bother about all that since we are really not talking about a healing technique at all. What we are talking about is a state of awareness that is so orderly, so completely restful, that healing takes place automatically and without effort. Try it for yourself. You'll be amazed.

Creating a Healing Event with the EuStillness Healing Technique

- Get your pre-test 0–10 (10 being unbearable, 0 being no symptoms).
- Place your hand(s) lightly on your partner.
- Ask your partner to let their mind wander anywhere it wants to go.
- Become aware of EuStillness.
- Continue for 2 to 3 minutes, then ask how your partner is feeling.
- Continue for another 2 to 3 minutes or longer until symptoms diminish.
- Get your post-test 0–10.

That's pretty much it. For both you and your partner's feedback I would recommend doing a pre-test and post-test. Before starting, ask them to grade their discomfort 0–10, 10 being unbearable. Don't forget to have them move that part of their body that hurts, and note their range of motion. Then, when you have finished the session, have them repeat the 0–10 test and to give you their number. In almost all cases the number will have diminished. And even if you don't see immediate results, most likely they will come later, within an hour or two or even longer. I've had partners who have called me days after our session together to say that the problem, even after years of discomfort, had completely disappeared.

It's up to you how long a session should last. Sessions can last from a few minutes to an hour, especially in chronic cases.

It is very important to note that you, as the initiator of the healing event, do not do anything. That is, after you become aware of EuStillness, you don't try to make healing happen. For instance, you don't need to have an intention for healing to take place. You don't need to direct energy or enlist any kind of outside help for healing to take place. This is possibly the hardest part of the Eu-Stillness healing procedure: not doing. Once you become aware of EuStillness ... don't do anything! And here is the reason why.

Your body already knows how to heal, doesn't it? It is the height of egoism for us to think that we know better than our bodies when it comes to healing. When you get a cut on your finger, how involved are you in the actual healing? Not at all, right? The inflammation response takes place and the platelets get where they need to be without your help. The scab forms and healing progresses, all without your intervention. Sorry, but when the conditions are right for healing, your body just doesn't need your help.

When you gently contact your partner and become aware of EuStillness you have created the perfect environment for healing. You are experiencing the deepest level of rest available to you at that time and, because they are there with you, your partner experiences that remarkably deep rest too. Now just enjoy EuStillness and let their body draw from that deepest healing harmony to create its own healing.

Don't misunderstand me. I'm not saying that you only need EuStillness for complete healing. It is just that becoming aware of EuStillness is the first and most important step. As I mentioned earlier, don't mix anything into the EuStillness Technique. Don't pray, create intentions, surround yourself with white light, or otherwise create positive energies. You can do all of that after you do the EuStillness Technique.

That does not mean that you should not follow accepted healing protocols to help things along. For instance, considering your tennis partner with the sprained ankle, you could elevate the foot, ice it, and wrap it with a bandage. All will help in the healing, but none will be effective without rest, and the deepest rest you can offer is awareness of EuStillness. So what I am saying is do everything that you can to help the healing process along, but do not add to or change in any way the EuStillness Technique. EuStillness is a must for any and all healing, as it provides the deepest rest.

This is especially true when you have enlisted the help of a healthcare professional in the healing. For instance, if you are seeing a medical doctor for hypertension, then follow his or her advice (always follow the advice of your healthcare professional when appropriate) and also do the EuStillness Technique. In this way you will heal more quickly and more completely. Additionally, any medication you take will work more effectively and the side-effects will be reduced. By the way, if you have blood pressure concerns, try this little experiment. Take your blood pressure before and after you do a 5-minute EuStillness session. You will find that in that short time your blood pressure will move toward normalization. The same is true with hypoglycemia or diabetes. Take your blood sugar before and after a EuStillness session and marvel at the results.

If you want to do the EuStillness Technique to heal yourself, it's really quite simple. I recommend doing your pre-test then sitting down and closing your eyes for 5 minutes or longer and just enjoy EuStillness. Then do your post-test. That's it; that's all you need.

At first, healing yourself with the EuStillness Technique may not seem as effective as when you do it with another person. That is because you are more emotionally involved, which frequently draws your attention away from EuStillness. Not to worry, with practice you will give up looking for specific results and just accept whatever comes naturally.

Healing from EuStillness takes place on a priority basis and will go where it's needed first. So you may find that not only is your primary concern being taken care of, but secondary problems will start to dissolve effortlessly on their own. It really is a quite remarkable process.

Emotional Healing With the EuStillness Technique

The EuStillness Technique works great for physical problems but is even that much more effective for emotional concerns. Here's how to conduct an emotional EuStillness session.

- Get your pre-test (1–10).

- Place your hand(s) lightly on your partner.

- Ask your partner to let their mind wander anywhere it wants to go.

- Become aware of EuStillness.

- Continue for 2 to 3 minutes then ask how your partner is feeling.

- Continue for another 2 to 3 minutes or longer until symptoms diminish.

- Get your post-test.

As you can see, emotional and physical EuStillness healing is virtually the same. Here is the major difference – and it is a big one. When you get your pre-test you do not want to know what your partner's emotional concern is. Let me repeat that. Don't ask and don't let them tell you what is bothering them. Even if they want to share, you don't want the extra baggage. Remarkably, the deep rest that they get during the EuStillness session will work whether you know what is bothering them or not. That is because their mind does the healing, not you. All it needs is a sufficient dose of stillness. That is what all of us need and very few of us are getting in this chaotic, fear-driven, goal-oriented world. OK I'll get off my soapbox, but I am serious about taking on their emotional concerns. Don't do it, not even to be polite. You don't need it and they don't need it. You are giving them what they need most: a chance to spend some quality time with you in EuStillness. That is the deepest healing and the best gift you can give anyone.

I want you to let your imagination run wild. Think of all the different ways you can use the EuStillness Technique to heal. Can you do it without touching? Can you do it over great distances? Will it work if the other person is asleep or in a coma? How does it work with children? What about healing your pets? Are the healing effects intensified in a group? Can I do the EuStillness Technique with trees or inanimate objects? Will it help with hunger and over-eating? How about sleeping and insomnia? Can I apply EuStillness to my financial worries?

You see, we have just scratched the surface of healing through EuStillness. I have written extensively about healing in my previous books, so there is no need to review that material here. My previous work revolves around Quantum Entrainment (QE), an extraordinary technique founded on awareness of Eufeeling. By learning the Eu-Stillness Technique – that is, by learning how to perceive the stillness within Eufeeling, you have learned a more insightful and potent lesson. Whenever you read the words "Quantum Entrainment" or QE in my other books, you can substitute instead EuStillness Technique. EuStillness includes but goes beyond Quantum Entrainment.

If you want only a single book from my past works that would give you the best bang for your buck, then I would recommend *The Kinslow System: Your Path to Proven Success in Health, Love, and Life*. This book includes QE experiences and techniques from all the previous QE books. Although it does not go as deeply into the philosophy, *The Kinslow System* does have additional experiences, applications, and material the other books don't have. You can find a full list of Kinslow System resources on our website at www.KinslowSystem.com.

I would encourage you to do at least one EuStillness healing every day. That could be for yourself or a partner, and your partner could even be in a different city or even on the other side of the world. (There, I've gone and answered one of the questions for you.) The more you do EuStillness for others, the more healing you will receive. I'm going to let you in on a little secret. When you do a EuStillness healing with another person, you always get

more than you give. And another thing, when you do Eu-
Stillness with another person, it intensifies EuStillness and
its healing effects. (Drat, I've gone and answered another
question for you, but then I never was really good at keeping a secret.) So spread it around as much and as often as
you like. Do we have a deal? Fantastic! Just don't forget, if
it isn't easy and it isn't fun, it isn't EuStillness. See you in
the Stillness ...

Main Points – Chapter 7

- Healing means reducing activity, or creating
  a deep enough rest so that reorganization in
  the injured area can take place.

- Rest is the universal healer. The deeper the
  rest, the deeper the healing. Awareness of
  EuStillness is the deepest rest we can attain.

- The initiator of EuStillness healing does
  nothing other than become aware of
  EuStillness.

- Your body already knows how to heal; all it
  needs is a deep enough rest.

- EuStillness awareness is the first step for any
  healing procedure.

- Do at least one kind of EuStillness healing a
  day: physical, emotional, remote, self, etc.

CHAPTER 8

THE NEGATIVE
SIDE OF POSITIVE
THINKING

"All this trying to make everything
right is a big part of what's wrong."

~ OLIVER BERKEMAN

Up to this point you and I have explored a number of liberating ideas. They have proven to be natural, simple, easy, and immediately applicable. For instance, the idea that you can clear your mind of thought, not in years but in seconds, flies in the face of current and traditional teachings. Or the fact that becoming aware of EuStillness, something you have always had, can quickly eliminate harmful emotions you may have been carrying around since childhood. How about the fact that you can now initiate a healing event in others with just a simple shift of your perception to EuStillness? We, you and I, have entered into a partnership to dispel outdated, debilitating paradigms that have been chipping away at our quality of life. Step by step you have proven these exceptional teachings to be true for yourself, haven't you?

I feel it necessary to point this out to you because without a doubt what we are about to explore has met with the deepest opposition despite everyone's experience to the contrary. And what is it that has the pseudoscientific community's panties in a twist? Why, that would be the negative effects of positive thinking.

When they talk about positive thinking, and I emphatically include under this umbrella "law of attraction" advocates, many take on an evangelistic fervor as if they are offering you the keys to the universe. They make you feel as though all you have to do is switch on positive thinking and the angels on high will spread rose petals on your path to material wealth and prosperity. Likewise, they tell you that the law of attraction means "like increases like" and positive thoughts can attract to them positive outcomes. They will tell you that this reasoning is based on solid principles of physics. Basically, they say, the law of attraction is telling us that our thoughts can control the material world. This may come as a surprise to many of you, but there is no "law of attraction" in physics or any other science. The whole positive thinking movement is scientifically baseless.

The most recent reincarnation of the idea that thoughts can control the material world comes out of the well-known, but frequently misinterpreted double-slit experiment in quantum mechanics. This classic experiment demonstrates that the outcome of the experiment is determined by what the observer measures. Briefly, if the scientist observed a photon in one way he found it to be a particle, and in another it presented as a wave. Now, I don't want to get too technical here, and it's not at all necessary in order to reach my objective. You can Google "double-slit experiment" and pick up the basics, but here's my point. You could say that the scientist controlled whether he observed a particle or a wave, but you can't say that he "created" the particle or the wave. The scientist seemingly influenced the outcome of the experiment by his observation of it, but in the end he was only observing what was already created. His observation determined whether he measured the photon as a particle or a wave, but he could not turn that particle or wave into a double-bacon cheeseburger. You see what I mean?

To further build on this misconception, the law-of-attraction aficionado proudly announces that if a scientist can control matter with his mind on the subatomic micro level, then we can control matter on the macro level of cars and Mars and jelly jars. This is a rather huge inductive leap with no foundation in experimental investigation. The scientist of the double-slit experiment was able to observe a single subatomic particle. Materializing your dream home is infinitely more complicated then observing a single photon. Your dream home is constructed of an unimaginable number of subatomic particles which form atoms which form molecules which then form the bricks, pipes, drywall, electrical wires, aluminum siding, etc., of your dream home. Are you truly capable of observing all of these particles in just the right way so that they materialize as your dream home? If so, would you think up a brand-new Ferrari for me? I'm just covering all my bases ...

"No," says the law-of-attraction believer, "it is the organizing power of the universe that does the work." That there is order in the universe is obvious. That we can bend that power to our individual will has yet to be shown. There may be a greater lesson to be learned, one of observation versus control. I rather like the position of the scientist in the double-slit experiment. He is an awed observer of that universal organizing power. Isn't that enough? From what emptiness springs our need to control every minute aspect of our world when the greatest joys afforded us have always been those spontaneous revelations of love and laughter accompanied with the realization that my world, our world, is beautiful just as it is?

Obviously our ability to imagine, plan, and control is inherent and necessary to our survival. It is the earmark of a healthy human, and has assured not only our existence but ascension to the apex of the animal kingdom. But there is a second kind of control, aberrant and born of dissatisfaction, disassociation, and fear. It is normal to want to free oneself from suffering. And if that suffering continues over a long enough time, it is common for that distressed mind to seek unrealistic and even detrimental relief. The control of the contented soul is giving, playful, and life-supporting. It lacks the frenetic sense of urgency, self-absorption, and hope that pervades a soul in suffering. The good news is that the suffering soul does not need to go outside of itself to relieve its torment. In fact, it cannot find permanent relief anywhere else but within. The misdirected mind, once on track, leaves behind that impulse and finds comfort in the present, no matter how chaotic or harsh it may appear.

If the positive-thinking movement is scientifically baseless, then why is it so popular? Does positive thinking work under more esoteric "cosmic" or spiritual laws beyond the reach of modern scientific reasoning? Well that certainly is the insinuation, but there is no proof of that either. So how does positive thinking work? The short answer is, it doesn't! At least it doesn't work the way it has been popularly presented.

There is more to be gained by exposing the inadequacies of positive thinking than you might think, and it takes only a little scratching below the surface to realize the real and practical benefits for ourselves. Shall we do that? Shall we throw out the useless and replace it with something practical that will actually work? Then let's get to it.

We will first look at the negative effects of positive thinking and then move on to create an actual positive perception that will ... well, let's just wait until we clear the complexities of positive thinking before we lay in our foundation for further fulfillment.

We have all heard of the wonderful results of positive thinking and the law of attraction. You know, think in just the right way to create the perfect partner or win the lottery. We hear about it a lot, but how often do you think it actually happens? Well as it turns out not very often at all, certainly not enough to be statistically significant. Let's look at it from the other side. How many times has the law of attraction been conjured up with no results? As it turns out, failure of the law of attraction way outweighs its successes. Isn't that your own experience? In actuality the law of attraction is no more effective at manipulating our world then is mere chance or happenstance. If it did work, everyone would be doing it and we would all be living utopian lives.

Why then do we hear so much about the successes of positive thinking? It's the yellow Volkswagen phenomenon. Picture yourself driving down the road when out of the blue your passenger says, "Did you know that the day after you see a yellow Volkswagen you will receive unexpected money?" All of a sudden you see yellow

Volkswagens everywhere, on the road, in parking lots, even in your dreams. Now, was it your lust for unexpected money that materialized yellow Volkswagens out of thin air? Some would say that seeing those yellow Volkswagens proved the law of attraction was hard at work in your favor. Or could it be that you were alerted to yellow Volkswagens and just became aware of what already existed? Remember Occam's razor, which holds that the hypothesis with the fewest assumptions is the one that is most likely to be true. Did your law of attraction positive thought wave-patterns reverberate throughout the universe inspiring yellow Volkswagen vibrations to manifest full blown and fully loaded in the left turn lane at the next stoplight? Or did your heightened Volkswagen awareness simply make you notice what had been there all along? Do you see how easily this can get out of hand? But there's more.

Reproducibility, that's what a scientific technique is all about. By following the same instructions you must be able to duplicate what others have produced. Despite all manner of anecdotal evidence to the contrary, positive thinking, including intention work, is not reproducible. Let's pick the most obvious example.

In 2007 a book was published that guaranteed its readers that the information within would provide "an incredible revelation that will be life-transforming for all who experience it". I do not like to unnecessarily point fingers so I will not name the book. That will be my "secret". This book, based on the law of attraction, became phenomenally successful – apparently a perfect example of the author's teachings. The author then wrote a follow-up book which, despite the notoriety of the first, was far and away less successful. Now my question is this: "Did the author have an intention for her second book to be *less* successful?" Do you see what I'm getting at here? Did the author, a master of the law of attraction, invoke that law to create a significantly less successful book or, despite her mastery of the law of attraction, was she unable to make it work? I'll let you be the judge.

If positive thinking were benign, a useless dalliance of the mind, then it would be nothing more than a frivolous waste of time. But positive thinking is *not* benign. Ironically, positive thinking can have negative psychological backlash. You may be surprised at this revelation, but when you understand the mechanism you will know it to be true from your own experience. Let's take a few minutes to explore these negative effects and how we can overcome them. Remember, our job is *not* to eliminate positive thinking. That would be ridiculous. Our job is to eliminate the negative effects of the improper application of positive thinking. And for that we have the perfect tool. But before we get to that, let's take a quick look at what others have to say about the negative effects of positive thinking.

A study by researchers Ayelet Fishbach from the University of Chicago and Jinhee Choi from Korea Business School found that when you stay focused on your goals, you *diminish* your ability to enjoy what you are doing. Less satisfaction in the doing translates to a decreased ability to reach your goal. Their subjects were asked to work out in a gym. One group focused on the goal, for instance running on a treadmill, while the other group, without a goal, just focused on the experience of the workout. The group that focused on their goal had more enthusiasm but less success than the non-goal-oriented group. Additionally, the goal-oriented group felt that the exercise was more of an effort than the other group. Apparently, keeping your eye is on the goal diminishes your ability to enjoy what you are doing right now. In essence you are living an illusion skewed toward a positive outcome rather than facing the present reality.

In her book *The Willpower Instinct*, Stanford University psychologist Dr. Kelly McGonigal, who has one of the most popular classes in Stanford history, tells us that making a resolution or affirmation makes us feel good at the moment, but creates an unrealistic or optimistic expectation of the future. It creates a kind of satisfaction or relaxation that does not allow us to have a realistic idea of the present and the future. They actually make us far less motivated to get back on track and reach our goals. When we fail to reach our goals we can feel guilty or frustrated. The harder we are on ourselves, the harder it is for us to be successful. It sets us up for a bigger fail.

Heather Barry Kapps and Gabriele Oettingen, conducting research out of New York University and the University of Hamburg, also found that positive thinking resulted in less energy and poor achievement. The reason cited for the poor achievement of generated positive thinking, "… [positive thinking] does not generate enough energy to pursue the desired future." But they didn't stop there. Oettingen had her subjects think about the realistic obstacles to achieving their goals. In essence, the test subjects injected a healthy dose of reality to balance the pie-in-the-sky positivity. In positive thinking parlance, this reality is considered negativity. What was the result? Oettingen's subjects who included possible obstacles to reaching their goals outperformed those participants who only focused on the possible positive outcome.

Negativity is a reality. Negativity has value. It does no good to deny its existence or try to neutralize its impact by playing the law-of-attraction game. Those who try to neutralize negativity not only find it a drain on spontaneous living but find it necessary to generate copious amounts of energy to maintain a mood of success in the face of continual failure. You will see a forced and frozen smile on their face and fear in their eyes. They know the force of evolution is working against them but don't know how to stop it. They don't know they shouldn't try. It's like trying to maintain the integrity of your sand castle when the tide is coming in.

There is a counterculture to positive thinking, a kind of hidden in plain sight non-movement slowly gaining momentum. At first I thought the negative thinking advocates were simply a backlash, a kind of sour grapes movement against the sucrose sweet teachings of positive thinking. But not at all, and you are going to love this. They have been around since the sandaled feet of the ancient Greeks beat a dusty path to the Parthenon. I am talking about the school of philosophy called Stoicism which blossomed shortly after the death of Aristotle. According to Oliver Burkman, author of *The Antidote: Happiness for People Who Can't Stand Positive Thinking*, the Stoic's ideal state of mind was inner peace, not exuberant happiness. And this is an important point. They were actually applying negativity to counterbalance the overtly optimistic, to settle somewhere in between. The Stoics sought through reason what Newton's third law of motion discovered through, well, motion. They were looking for equilibrium.

According to Burkman, "Rather than struggling to avoid all thought of these worst-case scenarios, they counsel actively dwelling on them, staring them in the face." The technique they employ is negative visualization. Here's how it works. When we find something that we enjoy or even love we soon acclimate to its presence and it does not offer us that same level of happiness. It doesn't matter if it's our brand-new whiz-bang, super-duper smart phone or our loving and always supportive partner, in a short amount of time our interest lessens and then our level of enjoyment drops. The object of happiness then fades into the background. Negative visualization dictates that we contemplate the loss of that entity. Negative visualization would have you picture what life would be like without your smart phone or your partner. When your increased awareness falls on that object of happiness it rejuvenates your interest and increases your level of enjoyment. Reminding yourself that you could lose something automatically increases your appreciation of it.

Negative visualization offers another more substantial advantage over positive thinking, and that is the reduction of anxiety. Positive thinking will have you visualize that you already have what you are seeking. Now, you not only have to energetically maintain that illusion but you have to combat the fear of losing it. This phenomenon is especially evident in people who are "always happy". They tend to overtly push hyper-happiness ahead of them with exaggerated beaming smiles like radar searching for sustenance. But their eyes forsake them. The muscles around their eyes are strained and pinched. Instead of the spontaneous spark of life, deep within their eyes you will find only bewilderment torched by fear. What is it they fear? They fear the loss of the illusion, something they never owned in the first place. Imagine how unsettling it is to fear losing something you never had in the first place.

Our fear of loss is almost always exaggerated. How many times have you worried about something going wrong and when it finally did it wasn't as bad as you had imagined? This is almost always the case. Negative visualization brings the actual loss into focus and reduces or eliminates the fear of the unknown. It gives you a more realistic vision of possibilities. The higher you build your castle in the air the farther you have to fall back to earth. The Stoics would have you live closer to reality right here on Earth. But as I have mentioned before, there is nothing wrong with having your head in the clouds as long as your feet are on the ground.

You could well ask, "How is the Stoics negative-neutralizing-positive approach any different from the positive thinker's positive-neutralizing-negative orientation?" There is a subtle distinction but an extremely important one for all who search for fulfillment. Positive thinkers want to replace negativity with positivity, a kind of denial of reality. Stoics, and a number of other systems that accentuate the negative, do not look to supplant positive emotions. Rather, they strive to recognize the reality that negative and positive both exist, and that the realization of such frees one from struggling to achieve happiness. In other words, they look for the still state that underlies and connects both worlds. The Stoics are searching for EuStillness.

I'm going to let you in on a little secret. Stoics and other negative-visualization advocates, law-of-attraction practitioners and other positive thinkers, as well as those minds stuffed full of the mundane, the magnificent, or even the magical, are all searching for the same thing: EuStillness. EuStillness is the ground state connecting, supporting, and inner-penetrating all worlds, negative and positive. In fact, when aware of EuStillness the contrast between negative and positive begins to soften. I guess a good analogy would be sugar cubes in water. Place a few inches of water in a tumbler. Drop in two sugar cubes: one represents negative and the other positive. Watch as the integrity of each cube dissolves first into each other and then, in time, disappearing into the water itself. What is called for is a way to resolve the apparent struggle between the forces of positive and negative. We are looking for some process or perception that allows you to know both positive and negative and, more importantly, the unifying essence, the glue that binds the two. Or, in the case of the sugar cubes, the water into which both the negative and positive cubes dissolve.

In the next chapter I will introduce you to the Coin Technique, a most remarkable process of perceiving your world in a way that will not eliminate negativity or positivity but harmonize them. The Coin Technique bridges the gap between negative visualization and positive thinking, empowering both and reducing each to its lowest common denominator, EuStillness. It opens the reality that all opposites dissolve in the oneness of stillness. Opposites are both separate and one.

Main Points – Chapter 8

- There is no "law of attraction" in science. The positive-thinking movement grounded on this law is scientifically baseless.

- The attempt to rely on outside entities for inner contentment is misdirected.

- Law of attraction techniques are not consistently reproducible.

- Positive thinking can have a negative psychological backlash.

- Our job is *not* to eliminate positive thinking. Our job is to eliminate the negative effects of the improper application of positive thinking.

- Negativity has value.

- Our fear of loss is almost always exaggerated.

- Negative visualization-advocates, law-of-attraction practitioners, as well as those minds stuffed full of the mundane, the magnificent, or even the magical, are all searching for the same thing: EuStillness.

- EuStillness is the ground state connecting, supporting, and inner-penetrating all opposites including negative and positive.

CHAPTER 9

THE COIN
TECHNIQUE

"Do, or do not. There is no 'try'."

~ YODA (*THE EMPIRE STRIKES BACK*)

The thing about the way most of us live is that we are either running away from or toward something. One of the driving biological principles is that life moves away from pain and toward pleasure. This is natural and quite evident with even just the most superficial observation. But let's look a little more closely at this phenomenon of not only pain and pleasure but all opposites.

Let's start with Newton's third law of motion: for every action there is an equal and opposite reaction. Motion means movement, which is activity, right? So Newton is telling you that activity has an equal and opposite element. You have already been introduced to this idea. Remember when we discussed that in order to stand up you must first push down, or to shoot an arrow forward you must first pull it back. And you will remember that after you pulled it back and before you let it go, the arrow had the quality of dynamic stillness, unmoving but charged with potential energy to spring forward and hit the target.

Because of the nature of your mind, you focus on movement first. This is a survival mechanism, a genetic predisposition recognizing that it is the motion that matters, the tiger in the weeds that will eat you. So your first impulse is toward motion. That is a good thing. But when you focus only on motion and ignore stillness, your life lacks for fullness. That is a not-so-good thing.

All life must rest. In fact, all creation must rest. That is an un-bendable law. Inherent and hidden in Newton's third law of motion is absolute stillness. I'll bet you never learned that in physics class. Even physicists have the tendency to entertain motion and ignore stillness. But when you have motion in one direction concurrent with equal motion in the other, what is inferred? Of course, that would be stillness. Ten units of positive force plus 10 units of negative force equals zero, doesn't it? Zero means no force, no movement. No movement is another way of saying stillness. So you see, Newton's third law of motion is built on the foundation of stillness.

The simplest building block of the universe, the wave, demonstrates this reality. Like a child on a swing, at the crest of the forward and backward swing each wave comes to a complete rest before moving again. Each period of rest in a wave is like the fully drawn arrow filled with dynamic stillness. It is this dynamic stillness that prepares the wave for its next leg of the journey. Those waves go on to interact with other waves to create our world. So you see, our world is a beautiful tapestry of stillness and activity.

We have been following Newton's laws for 350 years. It seems that we have edged out Newton in favor of the almost mystical laws of quantum physics. But not so.

Newton is not dead; he is just resting. It has been fewer than 100 years since the counterintuitive principles of quantum physics befuddled and then shocked the physics community. Even the fathers of this "new science" could not believe what they had discovered. Neils Bohr, a founding father and driving force behind this strange new science said, "Anyone who is not shocked by the quantum theory has not understood it." Werner Heisenberg, most noted for his uncertainty principle, told us, "... here the foundations of physics have started moving; and that motion has caused the feeling that the ground would be cut from science." What was bothering the scientists, and what has it to do with us?

Classical or Newtonian physics deals with the macro world, the world of our senses, of linear cause and effect. Newton felt that if we could gather enough data about an object or condition we could not only know its future but its past as well. Of course, except for the most elementary systems, this is not possible. We cannot know all the forces involved, all of the actions and reactions that have influence over even as simple an event as flipping on a light switch. Chaos theory's butterfly wing analogy probably best illustrates this point. You know, something like the energy created by the fluttering of a butterfly's wings in Taiwan can create a hurricane in Havana.

Until the advent of quantum physics, classical physics founded on Newton's laws dominated our thoughts and actions. It does so still today, as few disciplines including medicine, biology, chemistry, psychology, etc. have been able to integrate the principles and laws of quantum physics into their discipline. But, like any major shift in human consciousness, the realization of quantum physics appears to be trickling down into common everyday consciousness. Everywhere you look these days you have quantum this and quantum that, but when you look more closely you see that system or technique most likely follows Newtonian principles, or no established principles at all. Quantum Entrainment, best known for its rapid healing effects, is the notable exception. The initiator of QE, effortlessly aware of Eufeeling, simply steps aside and watches as subtle quantum mechanical forces reorganize (heal) physical and emotional discord. Despite the common usage of "quantum", quantum physics still remains mostly misunderstood.

What quantum physics is telling us is that a major shift in human consciousness can't trickle down, at least in the traditional sense. At the very core of quantum physics is the realization that life cannot be owned. Life is not a certainty – it is a probability, or, more accurately, both. Any thought, word, action, or object is at the same time a certainty and a probability. The pebble in the palm of your hand is a certainty only in the most superficial sense. You think you know the pebble. But what is its actual reality? Is it what you perceive with your senses? Is it a simmering soup of chemicals or a shimmering undulation of wave functions forming subatomic particles that blink in and out of existence at the speed of light? It is of course all of these things and more. And, it is less ... it is nothing.

The pebble is both being and becoming, dying and being reborn. Who among us can profess to know anything in its entirety? The possibilities are infinite in every direction and that is why certainty is an illusion. The closest we can come to accurately predicting the life of an atom, a pebble, or the evolution of our soul, is a probability. My favorite quote from Nisargadatta Maharajah, an Indian philosopher and teacher is, "Knowledge is ignorance." For as soon as we feel that we know a butterfly we imprison it within our mind, ending the process of becoming. There it becomes a memory isolated from its living, breathing reality. There it turns to stone.

So what are we to do? We must be open to both the apparent reality and the probability that it is becoming. How do we do that? We start by becoming aware of our own reality, the foundation upon which we will build. Who are we? Our bodies and minds are made of the same basic stuff as pebbles. Before they become subatomic particles or probability waves, they are still. Quantum mechanical theorist David Bohm calls that stillness *implicate order*. No machine can measure it but the human mind can experience it. When it does the mind and body in turn become still. This stillness is the progenitor of both being and becoming. From the vantage point of stillness we perceive the world before judgment and analysis and distorting emotions. Here the mundane becomes pregnant with potential. The pebble in the palm of your hand breathes in light and exhales love.

What I'm driving at here is this. We need to be at home in both worlds, conventional and quantum mechanical. We must rectify the world of opposites. The perception of absolute stillness, that is EuStillness, is woefully absent from our lives and that throws us out of balance. Culturing the perception of EuStillness brings with it a stability that goes far beyond "feeling good". EuStillness stabilizes the way we see our world. It brings harmony and balance to the fore, which directly affects how we interact with not only the world around us but within us. We find inner peace navigating quiet waters while the roiling world around us struggles to make meaning of it all.

So how does awareness of EuStillness directly impact your life? Awareness of the stillness from which activity is born allows you to see both sides of life more evenly. It fills in the potholes and straightens the road you are traveling. It makes your journey more meaningful and more fun. This shift of perception from opposites to unity quells the mind, organizes it, and frees it from attachment to things and thoughts. When you make this shift in perception your life immediately begins to drop its attachment to negative emotions or the "positive" procedures to overcome them. Duality dissipates quickly over time in the realization that negativity and positivity are ultimately one and the same.

When stillness is forgotten and you see only things and motion, your mind becomes fascinated at how those things interact with each other. But without stillness it doesn't remain an interested observer. Without the anchor of EuStillness your mind gets swept away by the current of action, reaction, and other opposites like weak and strong, old and young, good and bad, and right and wrong. Like the simple wave, each opposite in life is born of stillness and relies on stillness for its continued existence. Without the touchstone of EuStillness your knowledge of a thing is only partial at best. And that brings us to the point of this chapter.

Opposites by definition are conflicting and contradictory. They have no apparent common ground that unites them. So when you perceive opposites like weak and strong you naturally choose one over the other. You take a position of supporting one and denouncing the other, don't you? You don't even have to try. Before you know it you have taken sides. Now you must expend energy to support your position or repudiate the other side. Your life becomes a struggle between opposites and it's mostly subliminal. In most of us, going on just below the conscious level of our mind is a seething sea of warring opposites. It takes huge amounts of energy to live solely in a world of opposites.

If you don't believe me, try this simple experiment. Choose something you like, a place, a food, a person, and then take time for reflection. Examine why you like it. There has to be a reason, doesn't there? For instance you might say something like: I like green apples instead of the red ones because they are not as sweet and the color green feels better than red. If you come up with the answer, "I don't know" then the process for liking or disliking something is hidden from your conscious mind. In the mind infused with EuStillness there is a sense of oneness, a feeling that everything is just right just as it is. Then the realization comes: ultimately, there is no fight to be fought.

People who are aware of stillness in activity have a very different way of perceiving their world and it creates within them a sense of inner harmony and outer ease and success. Abraham Maslow, who you probably know from Maslow's hierarchy of needs, was a psychologist who studied healthy people. He found that there is a small percentage of people among us who perceive life much more often in EuStillness. Most of them do this naturally from birth. The rest of us are left to find EuStillness on our own. Maslow called these natural EuStillness-ers (I just made up a new word!) *transcenders*. Transcenders are fascinating people and there is a lot that we can learn from them. We will spend just a few minutes with them now but will enjoy greater intimacy with these remarkable people later in the book. I might even show you how to become one yourself, if you like.

Transcenders, according to Maslow, see stillness in all things while they function at the practical everyday level. This not only makes them more responsive to beauty but gives them a deeper sense of justice. In the world of the transcender, opposites are not two warring entities but more like two sides of the same coin. On the applied level they see the differences but can easily reconcile them on the unifying level of stillness.

So how would a transcender aware of EuStillness look at good and evil? Her perception of stillness would foster in her a sense of understanding that evil is unavoidable. Not only that, she would see, from her stillness vantage point beyond activity, that evil serves a function. She would intuitively know that the evil events of today can sow seeds of harmony, healing, and love in the future. Understanding the nature of evil, the transcender would strongly resist evil, not from a platform of fear, prejudice, and hate, but rather compassion, consideration, and understanding. The term "tough love" comes to mind.

If a poisonous snake were to find its way into her home, the transcender might return the snake to the wild where it no longer posed a threat to humans and could still perform its valuable role intended by Nature. Or, if removal were not possible, the transcender would have no qualms about killing the snake but she would do so with compassion and maybe just a touch of cosmic sadness. Stillness is a common ground, a spider web to which all things adhere. You cannot pluck a single rose but all of creation moves in sympathy.

And that brings us to the purpose of this chapter. I want to show you a special application of EuStillness that will quickly pacify the harshness and greatly reduce the energy drain that opposites impose upon you. In other words, I have found a way for you to appreciate the harmony within opposites and the joy that spontaneously accompanies that realization. I call it the Coin Technique.

You will be able to use the Coin Technique to dispel negativity in your life, or at least your attachment to it. You will also use this technique to dispel attachment to positivity. No, I am not suggesting that you stop enjoying life, not at all. Note I said "attachment" to positivity. Attachment is actually a form of negativity, isn't it? And when you have an attachment to positivity you defile the joy inherent in that person, place, or thing. Simply stated, you lose the ability to enjoy what you have right in front of you. Movement has a past and a future. Stillness is now. A suffering mind pushes away from negativity in an effort to embrace positivity but what it actually wants is a kind of neutrality, an even vision that accepts the present. In fact, when you are not swayed by positive and negative you have greater enjoyment of both. Of course, neutrality in this case is another word for stillness. And stillness in this case is another word for EuStillness.

You know, we can beat this thing to death with our intellect or we can just get on with learning the Coin Technique. What do you say? Are you ready to step out of the world of opposites and enjoy a little downtime? I am due for my daily shot of stillness. Why don't you join me ...?

If you have been regularly doing the EuStillness Technique, and especially the Stop-Hand Technique, you may have noticed that EuStillness, usually when you least expect it, drops in for a pleasant visit. When you take a moment to reflect you may even notice that EuStillness is always quietly present in the background supporting your life like a movie screen supports the images of a motion picture. Certainly this will be your perception as you continue to do these techniques.

The Coin Technique adds a wrinkle to what you have been practicing. It brings into conscious focus the opposing sides of an issue, event, concept, belief, relationship, etc., and infuses the apparent contradiction with the sameness of stillness. This perception brings balance to the conflict. Good and bad, right and wrong, strong and weak, young and old, all have common ground in EuStillness. Even if the conflict cannot be resolved outwardly, the perception of EuStillness dissolves inner conflict by showing that in essence both sides have a common ground, come from and continue within the same source. Realization of the unifying nature of EuStillness instills within you and intuitive depth of understanding beyond even logic and emotion. You come to know that despite the apparent fragmentation imposed by any conflict, freedom from duplicity resides in the simple perception of stillness. You know harmony where before existed only conflict.

Enough talk. Time for action ...

Before you engage the Coin Technique, first find a source of conflict in your life. It could be a disagreement with your partner or your boss. (In many relationships they are one and the same thing ... Take it easy, that's a joke.) You may disagree with a political decision or a human rights transgression. Or it could be as simple as whether you should clip your toenails now or wait another week.

Begin by sitting with your eyes closed and doing the EuStillness Technique. At first you may need 3 to 4 minutes of sitting quietly, but as stillness becomes more vibrant in your everyday awareness you will be able to do the Coin Technique pretty much anytime, anywhere. Once you are enjoying a firm awareness of EuStillness you are ready to begin the Coin Technique.

The Coin Technique

- Aware of EuStillness, bring your conflict to mind. Become aware of the situation in general, a kind of overview of the problem.

- Become aware of the problem and EuStillness.

- Now, entertain the positive things about your conflict. What is good about it?

- Become aware of what emotions you are feeling.

- Become aware of the positive elements and emotions and EuStillness.

- Entertain the negative things about your conflict, what you don't like about it.

- Become aware of what emotions you are feeling.

- Become aware of the negative elements and emotions and EuStillness.

- Now, become aware of 1 to 3 things that you might be able to do that would resolve the conflict. Take time to let your mind play with the possibilities, a kind of directed daydreaming. These solutions do *not* have to be realistic. Maintain a sense of playfulness. Have fun with the possibilities.

- Become aware of the resolution of the conflict and EuStillness.

- Become aware of 1 to 3 things that are interfering with the resolution of the conflict.

- Become aware of the hindrances to resolution and EuStillness.

- Become aware of the negative side of the conflict and the positive side of the conflict at the same time and become aware of EuStillness.

- Become aware of your Eufeeling (peace, joy, bliss, etc.) for 1 minute or so.

- Now, just let your mind wander wherever it wants to go, occasionally returning to EuStillness (2 to 3 minutes).

It's important to know that the goal of the Coin Technique is *not* to resolve a particular conflict. The object of the Coin Technique is to perceive unity in apparent diversity and conflict. Do you see the difference? We can never know how a conflict will be resolved. The forces bearing on any event are infinitely varied and ongoing. Everything is always changing. What works today is ineffective tomorrow. What you believe today you may not believe tomorrow. Isn't that true? Think back over your life. How many times have you completely believed in the efficacy of a person, philosophy, or system only to leave it behind in favor of its opposite. It turns out that in the relative world nothing is reliable. So we need consistency, something we can rely on. The only thing that is reliable is nothing, the nothing of absolute stillness. Perceiving EuStillness in the field of opposites, especially where we see conflict, gives us that solid foundation. Through our perception of Eufeeling we develop a sense of constancy and harmony within the world of warring opposites. EuStillness and its loving child Eufeeling provide for us that rock solid foundation.

After each step of the Coin Technique you are asked to become aware of EuStillness. This enlivens your perception of stillness within the outside world. This alone will relieve you of great fear and anxiety, guilt, anger, and sadness. Secondary to becoming aware of the unifying presence of all creation the Coin Technique will actually help you resolve specific conflicts within your life. As I have just mentioned, this cannot be a goal. When you do the Coin Technique with the idea that you will create a specific result, it will only backfire. We will spend a good deal of time on this very topic in the next chapter, but for now just do the Coin Technique without any expectations. Do it regularly. You can tack the Coin Technique onto the end of your EuStillness technique practice, or just do it when the mood strikes you. With practice you will be able to do this with your eyes open while you are in the midst of your everyday activities.

Make sure you do the Coin Technique just as it has been laid out for you above. The order is important. At first you may have to stop and refer to the Coin Technique instructions, but very quickly you will have the order in mind and the routine established.

There is an abridged version of the Coin Technique that I would like to share with you. You can get in the habit of doing this several times throughout the day whenever there is a pause in your schedule. Here's how it goes ...

The Coin Technique (Abridged)

- Become aware of EuStillness.
- Become aware of a person, place, or thing.
- Become aware of what you like about that person, place, or thing.

- Become aware of EuStillness.

- Become aware of what you don't like about that person, place, or thing.

- Become aware of EuStillness.

- Become aware of the person, place, or thing, its positive and negative attributes, and EuStillness, all three at the same time.

- Become aware of your Eufeeling.

OK, now that you are armed with the Coin Technique and are poised to destroy duality wherever it raises its ugly head, you are probably wondering why I called it the Coin Technique. Pretty simple really, it refers to the saying "there are two sides to every coin" meaning that every created thing has its opposite expression. Let's take the example of negative and positive. Let's say you have a gold coin with "N" for negative embossed on one side and "P" representing positive on the other side. Both letters are formed from the gold, aren't they? Each stands for something different but in essence they are both part of, and dependent upon, the coin. Without the coin the N and P could not exist. Without EuStillness negativity and positivity could not exist. Focusing only on the N or the P limits your appreciation of the wholeness of life. With the Coin Technique you have access to the currency of living and loving. Now get out there and spend, spend, spend!

Main Points – Chapter 9

- All life must rest.

- It takes huge amounts of energy to live solely in a world of opposites.

- Awareness of EuStillness allows you to see both sides of life more evenly.

- Aware of EuStillness, perception shifts from opposites to unity freeing your mind from attachment to things and thoughts.

- Awareness of EuStillness in activity brings with it a sense of inner harmony and outer ease and success.

- The Coin Technique will actually help you resolve specific conflicts within your life, but this cannot be the goal. Resolution of conflict comes from perception of the unifying and harmonizing influence of stillness within opposites.

- Do the Coin Technique regularly. With practice you will be able to do it anytime, anywhere.

CHAPTER 10

THE SECRET LIFE
OF TRANSCENDERS

*"Self-actualization is the intrinsic growth
of what is already in the organism, or more
accurately, of what the organism is."*

~ABRAHAM MASLOW

They live among us, quiet, unassuming, powerful be-
ings. Governed by separate laws than you and I, they insidiously infect the general population with alien mores
and uncommon insight. They are of us yet apart from
us. They are impossible to identify unless you have the
cypher. Your boss might be one. Your neighbor might be
one. You might be one! They are *transcenders*.

I know this sounds like something out of a cheesy sci-
ence-fiction movie, but it is true. There are people who
look and sound like us but inside, where their thoughts
and motivations and love for life are forged, they are wholly different. In each generation examples of their gentle
hand on the helm of humanity can be felt steering us
toward an ever-deepening realization of who we are and
what we are capable of being.

Transcenders were most clearly defined in the 20th century by humanistic psychologist Abraham Maslow. You may remember Maslow from your high school psychology class. He is most recognized for his "hierarchy of needs" which theorizes that we must fulfill our more basic needs before we can go on and fulfill our "higher" needs. For instance, if your boat has capsized and you find yourself drowning, you are at that moment not concerned about finding a better job. The physiological need for breathing to live takes immediate precedence over the safety need of earning enough money to live on.

Let me take a moment here and refresh your memory, as this hierarchy is helpful in understanding where you may be and what you are capable of. We will round out this picture of where you came from, where you are, and where you were going when we later look at George Land's theory of transformation. It's comforting and even helpful to know where you are going, but the "how" of fulfilling your greatest potential is paramount. That is why you are reading this book. The EuStillness Technique is the bridge between theory and practical application.

Maslow's Hierarchy of Needs
From lowest to highest:

- Physiological: breathing, food, water, sex, sleep, homeostasis, excretion

- Safety and security: body, employment, resources, morality, the family, health, property

- Love/belonging: friendship, family, sexual intimacy

- Esteem: self-esteem, confidence, achievement, respect of others, respect by others
- Self-actualization: morality, creativity, spontaneity, problem solving, lack of prejudice, acceptance of facts

You are going to love this. Along with the ascending hierarchy of needs there is also an ascending scale of grumbling! Grumbling is a kind of low-grade complaining. Basically, you grumble when you feel something is missing or needs adjusting. Maslow says man will always grumble. So now you can actually determine where on the scale of needs a person is by how he verbally vents his frustrations. You can monitor your own progress as you leave the lower needs levels behind. As your lower needs are satisfied you begin to grumble at a higher level. Isn't that an interesting concept? And yes, even transcenders grumble. Let's take a look at the different levels of grumbling.

- Low Grumbling – physiological and safety needs

  1. survival – food, shelter, clothes, illness, indignities, abuse, prejudice, cruelty, death related to survival

  2. safety – work issues, financial issues, planning for the future, indignities, abuse, prejudice, cruelty, related to safety

- High Grumbling – belonging and self-esteem needs

1. belonging – being misunderstood
   or accused, racial/gender profiling,
   comparing you to others

2. self-esteem – dignity, self-respect, respect
   for others, autonomy, feelings of worth,
   praise and rewards, receiving recognition
   for work

- Meta-Grumbling – self-actualization/
  transcender

   1. self-actualizer – inefficiencies in free flow
      of work, inaccuracies in information and
      communication

   2. transcender – need for truth, perfection,
      beauty, imperfection of the world,
      injustice to others

It is in the last, or highest human need for self-actualization that we are most interested. What world does a
self-actualizer live in? She experiences profound moments
of love, understanding, happiness, and bliss. She feels
more alive and whole and tuned in to universal harmony.
She naturally values goodness and truth and fair play. She
has "being" awareness, realizing that everything is perfect
just as it is. Maslow calls these experiences B-values, the
"B" standing for being, a sense of oneness or unboundedness. Another word for being is stillness, which you are
now familiar with. You see, you are already strengthening
your self-actualization.

There are different degrees of experience within the
self-actualization group. Some self-actualizers experience
the B-values briefly and infrequently. We can refer to these

people as self-actualizing non-transcenders. Self-actualizing non-transcenders are realistic, accepting, spontaneous, natural, problem-centered, have a need for privacy, rely on inner self-satisfaction, and they have peak experiences. Exemplifying the self-actualizing non-transcenders group, Maslow submits Eleanor Roosevelt, Harry Truman, and Dwight D. Eisenhower.

The peak experience is unique in human experiences and is often referred to as a "spiritual" experience. When you have a peak experience you have feelings of limitlessness, of ecstasy, wonder, and awe. Your sense of time and space is altered. You may have a simultaneous feeling of great power, helplessness, and cosmic nurturing all rolled into one beautiful realization that you are both within the world and beyond it.

Now take a moment and think back over the experiences you had while practicing the techniques opened to you in this book. Did you at some time have a feeling of limitlessness, or was your sense of space and time altered? You can certainly say that was true when you looked beyond your thoughts during the Nothing Technique. What did you feel when you did the Eufeeling Technique? Did you feel a sense of peace or joy or unconditional love? Perhaps you felt nurtured or protected, as if you had stepped out of the onslaught of everyday living into your own safe world. You may also have noticed a great sense of expansion, a sense of existing unexpressed power when you did the EuStillness Technique. You may have perceived that things around you felt more alive, softer, more friendly. You may have felt that universal stillness within, leaving you content and comfortable with who you are and your place in this universe. Or you may have just had an overwhelming sense of well-being and "just rightness".

You may have only had one of these experiences for a moment or two, but that is more than 99% of your burdened brethren. Every time you experience EuStillness you open the door even wider to the light of enlightenment, the reality of becoming fully human. Maslow estimated that self-actualizers represent between 2% – ½% of the world's population. He confessed that the number is probably closer to ½% but without more exact measuring tools it is impossible to know for sure.

Maslow's theories have been in place for some 70 years, but the idea of self-actualization is almost as old as thinking man himself. Self-actualization goes by many names: self-realization, self-awareness, illumination, nirvana, bodhi, satori, moksha, even EuStillness – but by far the most common and widely used term is *enlightenment.* When referring to Maslow's work I will use self-actualization, but in general I will use enlightenment or EuStillness.

Just as Maslow noted, there are different degrees of self-actualization or enlightenment, and I will clearly define these variances of higher perception in the next chapter. For now let us concern ourselves with the overall value of this higher level of human functioning. Let's return to Maslow's peak experience.

Peak experiences remove your neurotic symptoms and allow you to view yourself in a more healthy way. When you self-actualize, you view other people and your relationship to them in a healthier way. Peak experiences release within you spontaneity, expressiveness, and creativity. They help you view life in general as being more whole and being more worthwhile. As you may have already found out, your practice of the EuStillness Technique and the Coin Technique encourages peak experiences.

When you have a peak experience that lasts a long time, it is called a plateau experience. Plateau experiences can last for hours, days, or even months; those who have plateau experiences are called transcenders. Transcenders epitomize the essence and the end of humanity, at least at this point in our evolution. Transcenders are subtler, softer souls infused with the stillness of being. They are the lighthouses of each generation and the rocks upon which the ignorance of the common man is splintered. They are most times unobtrusive, quietly affecting our world more through insight and order than through proclamations and demonstrations. They are not limited to culture, geography, education, religion, or race. You will find as many of them in business, education, and the political arena as you will amongst intellectuals, poets, and spiritual leaders. Maslow's 20th-century examples of transcenders are Aldous Huxley, Albert Schweitzer, Martin Buber, and Albert Einstein. Following is an excerpt of transcender qualities from Maslow's posthumously published book, *The Further Reaches of Human Nature.*

Qualities of a transcender:

- For transcenders, peak experiences and plateau experiences become the most important things in their lives.

- They speak easily, normally, naturally, and unconsciously the language of Being.

- They perceive the sacred within the secular.

- They are much more consciously and deliberately motivated by truth, beauty, goodness, and unity.

- They seem to somehow recognize each other and come to almost instant intimacy and mutual understanding even upon first meeting.

- They are more responsive to beauty.

- They are more holistic about the world. Thinking in our "normal" stupid or immature way is for them an effort, even though they can do it.

- They are lovable, revered, producing the thought: "This is a great man."

- They are innovators, discoverers of the new. Transcendent experiences and illuminations bring clearer vision of the B[eing]-values.

- They are prone to a kind of cosmic-sadness over the stupidity of people, their self-defeat, their blindness, their shortsightedness, their cruelty to each other.

- Mystery is attractive and challenging rather than frightening. Transcenders are somewhat apt to be bored by what is well known.

- They are more "reconciled with evil". They have a greater compassion with it and a more unyielding fight against it.

- Transcendence brings with it the "transpersonal" loss of ego.

- They are more apt to be profoundly spiritual in either the theistic or nontheistic sense.

- They find it easier to transcend the ego. They have strong identities, are people who know who they are, where they are going, what they want, what they are good for in accordance with their own true nature.

- They have more of the fascinations that we see in children who get hypnotized by the colors in a puddle, or raindrops dripping down a window pane, by the smoothness of skin, or the movements of a caterpillar.

- They perceive things in a more miraculous way, more perfect, just as it should be.

- They experience more wholehearted and un-conflicted love, acceptance, expressiveness, rather than the more usual mix of love and hate that passes for "love" or friendship or sexuality or power, etc.

- They may actively seek out jobs that make peak experiences and B-cognition more likely. They fuse their work and play. They get paid for what they would do as a hobby anyway, for doing work that is intrinsically satisfying.

To recap our terms:

- Non-transcender – member of any group below self-actualizing. Rarely if ever has peak experience.

- Self-actualizer– early stages of self-actualizing group. Peak experiences.

- Transcender – highest level in self-actualizing group. Plateau experiences. Includes the self-actualizer.

Looking at Maslow's hierarchy from the physiological needs through the esteem needs, the non-transcender is driven by deficiency. He feels a sense of loss, as if something indescribable but vital is missing from his life. This sense of loss rarely surfaces, but when it does he finds himself asking, "Is this all there is to life?" Usually this longing remains silent, insidiously overseeing every thought, word, and action he performs. In many this lack manifests as a sense of urgency, an almost frantic effort to fill the void with friends and possessions, money and power. This single drive has created nations of workaholics all in the name of progress. Others sense this hopeless emptiness and become poorly motivated or just "average", living lives of mediocrity. Still others become depressed or distorted and go on to create atrocities against society. All are examples of living the lower levels of humanity. The further we move away from our Self (EuStillness), the sicker we become and the more aberrant and frenetic is our behavior.

So what is it that the transcenders have that the non-transcenders don't? Succinctly stated, non-transcenders lack awareness of the silent side of life, of their own inner and unbounded essence. They lack awareness of EuStillness. Their efforts are directed outward toward possessing those very things that deepen the vastness of the void. Even when they decide they need to experience inner calm, they attack it like a dog on a bone. They assail stillness as if it were an object to be possessed rather than an innocent perception of non-locality. Most non-transcenders have neither the interest nor the patience to explore their inner realms. Those who do, because of misinterpretation and unqualified instruction, devote much time and effort to a process that is as instantaneous as it is natural and openly available. Even after years of dedication to achieving self-actualization, only meager movement in that direction is realized. However, the Eu-Stillness Technique does away with all the toil and hassle that have traditionally been associated with meditation or self-actualization techniques. Now anyone from any level of life can pick up from where they are and have a peak experience immediately. As awareness opens to essence, EuStillness literally begins to fill in the spaces with stillness, opening our perception to the beauty that we are. The EuStillness Technique ushers us instantly into the realm of self-actualization. We become immediate transcenders for a few moments or for a few hours. But as we continue our romance with EuStillness, it blossoms ever more fully. No matter from where you start, the EuStillness Technique can be integrated into your lifestyle with the utmost ease, and EuStillness integrated into your life with the utmost speed.

It is my opinion that at this point in our evolution most transcenders are born, not made. They come into this world already radiating their inner light. Many transcenders have no idea what they are or the power they possess. They think they are like everyone else, and they are given no reason to believe otherwise. Their parents, teachers, and even their peers may all be non-transcenders. These transcenders are taught to see life through the lens of deficiency rather than affluence. They are internally conflicted and can't figure out why. They feel estranged to the common man. They acquire a kind of love-hate relationship. They love and in return receive the fear and pain that non-transcenders inadvertently inflict. From a place of greatest humility they often find themselves thinking, "If others could just be more like me the world would be a wondrous place." And they would be right.

For some of you, just reading these words will be like cool water to a thirsty man. They bring great relief and joy. To understand why you have been struggling is a great freedom. Now you understand why you have always felt like you were swimming upstream against the current of commonality. Now you can stop trying to be what others want you to be. Now you can begin to listen to the inner whisperings of harmony and love that you have been denying since childhood. You are not sick, distorted, or peculiar. You no longer have to hide Self from yourself. Now you will open to your own inner light and begin, tentatively at first but with greater intensity, to share your special light with us all.

As you practice the techniques in this book and Eu-Stillness becomes more lively in your awareness, you will feel more at home with yourself. You will gain more confidence and become less defensive. Compassion and empathy will begin to well up within, transmuting into more patience and appreciation for the human condition. When you occasionally read through the list of transcender qualities above you will find more and more of them stealing into your awareness. Your world will be as it has always been, only richer, more supportive, and friendly. You will stop trying to attain EuStillness and just enjoy it for what it is: the pure reflection of your inner fullness.

With extra energy and a healthy dose of the non-expressed kind of universal love, you will naturally be compelled to help others. Helping can be hazardous and you may have had some bad experiences that have driven you in the other direction. After all, disharmony and disquiet is the nature of fear-driven non-transcenders. You only have to look around both here and abroad. With so much incredible potential in every area of human endeavor, we still manage to create so much conflict and suffering. Please don't get me wrong. I am not trying to emphasize the negative side human existence. It really doesn't need my help, but that's not my point. A transcender helps harmonize humanity just by his very existence.

If you doubt my word, then let me point out the healing you created when you were aware of EuStillness. Transcenders are like transducers. They become aware of their inner essence and reflect it outward into the world. You don't have to raise a banner or pen a proclamation. You don't even have to leave your house. The coherency that you create when you are aware of EuStillness radiates beyond any and all boundaries, gently influencing even those ignorant of self-actualization.

While the EuStillness Technique has value for all non-transcenders, the lower we go on Maslow's scale the less EuStillness is able to be is appreciated. You will find precious little time for EuStillness if a bear is chasing you up a tree. Likewise, people struggling to put food on the table or feel loved or appreciated are not so interested in what seems to be abstract and impractical. Oddly enough, awareness of EuStillness can help significantly in overcoming financial difficulties or realizing inner self-worth. As many of my readers have discovered, the EuStillness Technique is remarkably effective at enabling one to fulfill one's esteem needs, inviting them into the realm of self-actualization. The incredible thing is, if they don't want to do it for themselves you can do the EuStillness Technique for them, at least momentarily. During the EuStillness session they can be open to a peak experience, but in the end they will have to experience EuStillness for themselves. While doing the EuStillness Technique for someone else is a temporary fix, the good news is you will always get more out of it when you give it away.

By the way, it's is impossible to tell if someone is a transcender by his actions or intentions. Don't get caught up in trying to determine if someone is a transcender or not. This is most often an egocentric exercise and never fruitful. As Bertrand Russell was fond of saying, when you compare yourself to someone else you either get a false sense of security or insecurity, and neither is constructive. Your concern should be with infusing your own actions and intentions with stillness. Be ready to help where you can, but otherwise leave each of us to our own evolution. It just works out best that way.

As love for your Self grows it is natural to want to share that purest of perceptions with others. To my way of thinking, the best overall gift you can give someone is to introduce them to their Self, lifting their perception beyond the mundane to the miraculous. This is not an esoteric teaching savored by a chosen few, not by a longshot. The EuStillness Technique is so simple, fast, and practical that as soon as you are beyond the claws of that bear, EuStillness is just a thought away. Like a magnet brought to scattered iron filings, EuStillness creates order out of scattered thinking, stilling your mind and steadying your body, better preparing you to evade the jaws of any dilemma.

OK, we are zinging right along and before we explore the three phases of transformation that all life must go through to grow and prosper, and before you learn how to apply those steps to your life, I want to spend just a few minutes with you in the next chapter looking at the six levels of awareness. I think it would be good for us to look especially at the last two levels of awareness which correspond to the perceptions that transcenders have. OK then, see you in the next chapter.

Main Points – Chapter 10

- The self-actualizer "peak experiences" are profound moments of love, understanding, happiness, and bliss. He has "being" awareness, realizing that everything is perfect just as it is.

- The different degrees of experience range from the brief and infrequent peak experiences of self-actualizers to the longer-lasting plateau experiences of transcenders.

- The EuStillness Technique encourages peak experiences and plateau experiences.

- More than 99% of the world's population are deficiency-oriented, driven by frustration and fear.

- Fewer than 1% of the world's population are transcenders motivated by truth, beauty, and unity. They are lovable, innovators and discoverers who perceive the sacred within the secular.

- The EuStillness Technique is a new technology with ancient roots that offers the opportunity for all peoples to become transcenders.

CHAPTER 11

THE SCIENCE OF ENLIGHTENMENT:

How to Become Fully Human

"Knowing others is wisdom, knowing yourself is Enlightenment."

~ LAO TZU

You are sitting in a completely dark room. Your window is open to the night and the sun is beginning to rise. As the faint light of approaching dawn enters your room, you look down at your feet and you see a coiled snake ready to strike. Your breath catches in your throat. "Is the snake dangerous? Is it poisonous?" Your muscles tense and you are ready to take flight when the fear flashes in your mind that the snake may strike at any movement. With no way of knowing you sit unmoving, barely breathing. The sun continues to rise and more light filters into the room. You see the head of the snake and it is not looking directly at you. Your muscles relax a little and your breath deepens slightly. The sun breaks the horizon and floods the room with golden light, and in that revealing brightness you see that your snake is in reality a coil of rope. A flood of relief and joy wash over you and you are free of fear. You are rejoicing the pure experience of being alive.

What you just experienced in the few minutes that it took for darkness to give way to light was a rocket ride from the lowest physiological and survival needs into the exultation of transcendent self-actualization. How was that achieved? In the presence of ever-increasing light you maintained an acute perception of your condition.

The story of the coiled rope is an analogy for our own psychological evolution, but it also contains within it the ingredients for complete transcendence: perception and awareness.

Awareness and perception change with each state of human consciousness. But of the two, awareness is paramount. Imagine being without awareness. What would you have? Obviously, the answer is nothing. You certainly would not be able to perceive a thing without awareness. In the coiled rope analogy, you are perceiving mainly through your sense of sight. Awareness is to being as light is to seeing. Without light, sight does not exist. Without awareness we do not exist. Right now I would like us to take a few minutes to look at the six levels of awareness, how they interact, and how they affect your quality of life.

The six major states of awareness are waking, dreaming, deep sleep, pure awareness, EuAwareness, and EuStillness awareness.

Each major state of awareness is different from the other. Each state has its own physiological and psychological rules. Pertaining to the first four, waking through pure awareness, you can only experience one state of awareness at a time. In other words, if you are awake you are not asleep, if you are dreaming you are not in pure awareness. Minor states of awareness like daydreaming and hypnosis are variations and not considered one of the major states.

Let's start with the first three: waking, dreaming, and deep sleep. These really need very little introduction, as every healthy human experiences these three states of awareness regularly. What they may not realize is that each state of mental awareness has a physiological corollary. For instance, when you are in the waking state your mind is active and so is your body. When you are in deep sleep your mind is inactive and your body is very rested. In terms of physical and mental activity, when you are dreaming you are somewhere in between waking and deep sleep. While dreaming your mind is not as active as when you are awake, but more active than when you are in deep sleep. Your body is also more rested than when you are awake but not nearly as rested as when you are deeply asleep.

Pure awareness was discovered clinically by Dr. Robert Keith Wallace. In March 1970 he published a paper in *Science* magazine establishing the existence of pure awareness. (Wallace called pure awareness a "wakeful hypometabolic physiologic state", but I think we will stick with our "pure awareness" for obvious reasons.) When compared to the first three states, waking, dreaming and deep sleep, pure awareness is unique. When you are aware of pure awareness your mind is absolutely still and yet you are wide awake. Additionally, your body is actually more deeply rested then when you are in deep sleep. That is why when earlier you did the Nothing Technique and experienced pure awareness, even for just a moment or two, you quickly experienced relaxation and inner peace. Spiritual leaders of every generation have been adamant in their teaching of pure awareness as essential for our spiritual well-being. But this is just the beginning of becoming a transcender, of becoming fully human.

I discovered a unique and quick way to seamlessly merge the waking state with pure awareness to create a fifth major state. For you this fifth major state of awareness has the advantage of providing you with a wide-awake mind and a very rested body while you go about your daily activities. It's like being in a light meditative state while you shop for peanut butter and rutabagas, get your teeth cleaned, gossip with your neighbors over the backyard fence, or balance your checkbook. No, you don't become a Zen-like zombie; quite the contrary. You become more responsive and more animate. Rather than being burdened with the internal dialogue of "should I or shouldn't I?", you have more fun just being you. It pops you from wherever you are on the needs scale directly into the early phases of self-actualization. And it delivers greater clarity and depth of perception if you are already self-actualizing. I call this fifth state of awareness *EuAwareness*.

EuAwareness is not new. It has been around since the first anatomical human transcended his lower needs and began self-actualizing. In my mind, I see a caveman, let's call him Uug-Lug, sitting at the mouth of his cave, head deeply bowed, contemplating the greatest mystery of his day, "where did my belly button come from?" Or his wife Sug-gug, contemplating what life would have been like had she married her old boyfriend Justin, who invented the wheel and spends three months a year in his summer cave in the Catskills. OK, I digress, my apologies.

My point is this: EuAwareness has been around a very long time and was probably much more prevalent when we had more time. Uug-Lug and his contemporaries only had to work 3 or 4 days a week to survive. That means that they had 3 or 4 days a week to contemplate their navels, watch the wind ripple the waters of a placid lake, or sit quietly on a log absorbing the sounds, sights, and smells of an ancient forest. Today time has become our opponent. We put so much effort into meeting our next deadline that we have left a vital part of ourselves behind: EuAwareness.

The teachings of the ancient masters are true but the technology is outdated. It was useful for a less hectic age. Most of us don't have 3 or 4 days a week to do with as we please. Those of us who do squander it, caught up in the fragmented, flashing world of terabytes and neon lights. It's no wonder that fewer than 1% of us are self-actualizing. We've got our priorities upside-down. But that's not really our fault. We have been raised in a fear-driven, deficiency-oriented world, a world that places great emphasis on doing and becoming rather than being. Both are necessary but must be balanced. Up till now, our only alternative has been to sequester ourselves, insulating our awareness in the cloaks of time-consuming spiritual philosophies and practices. With the introduction of the EuStillness Technique, EuAwareness can be cultured, nurtured, and integrated into our busy lives without greatly sacrificing our commitment to the God of Time.

EuAwareness is the beginning stage of enlightenment. A person experiencing EuAwareness roughly parallels the peak experiences of a self-actualizer. People in EuAwareness begin to blossom as the individuals they were meant to be. Their gifts and talents untangle themselves from the constricting vines of doubt, anxiety, and guilt. EuAwareness repairs the apparent rift that opposites impose on us. The Eu-aware are at the same time more creative and analytical, more spontaneous and calculating, more expressive and reserved. They are self-sustaining, self-satisfied, and self-assured, which lays the foundation for healthier relationships. They are more natural, more supportive, and more loving than their pre-Eu-aware selves could manage. In short, they are a purer reflection of the inner essence that makes them, and all of us, human.

The mind of the Eu-aware inhabits a special space. It is quietly aware, frequently looking at the world through the innocence and awe of the child's eye. They become more attuned to the inner energetic worlds and are able to apply this abstract knowledge in a practical way to the corporeal world. These are the realms frequented by the great minds like Socrates and da Vinci and Einstein. Each radio station on the dial has its own frequency. Each Eu-aware individual expresses her distinctive talent at the "frequency" that best suits her. She doesn't try to sing country music when she is a classical violinist. To take the analogy a little further, da Vinci might be a favorite classical hits station while Einstein might host a Science Friday type program. Socrates, of course, would be the star of talk radio, deeply questioning his guests and stirring up controversy. Each Eu-aware becomes the music he was meant to be. He finds his proper place, then proceeds to enlighten and inspire the rest of us.

Perceptually, the Eu-aware individual is in for a treat. In EuAwareness you actually perceive the world as a softer, friendlier, more loving place. You begin to shape a kinship with all created things. The boundaries that define one thing from another begin to dissolve in a kind of diffuse liveliness accompanied with a gentle adoration for anything manifest. The Eu-aware fall in love with life.

Then, a beautiful process is set into motion. As your perception in EuAwareness continues to refine, you begin to appreciate what you see. This appreciation opens your heart and you begin to experience the unhindered flow of unbounded love. Unbounded love, reflecting back from every created thing, opens your heart more fully. The process continues, refined perception generating love, love purifying perception as each petal of your self-actualizing Eu-aware life unfolds in EuAwareness. In time, your perception opens to the deepest expressions of life while your heart opens to the broadest expressions of love. With cultured heart and refined perception you poise on the brink of brilliance. You are ready for oneness, the realization that everything in your domain is the product of an all-permeating singularity: stillness.

In EuAwareness you begin to intuit an underlying unity between all things. In EuStillness that underlying unity becomes a direct perception. At first, as you may have already experienced by doing the EuStillness Technique, there appears to be stillness somehow embedded in everything around you: the objects, the activities, and even your own thoughts and emotions. In EuAwareness you enjoy each pearl that life presents you for its own luster. In EuStillness you become aware of the thread that binds each pearl, appreciating the wholeness of the necklace.

Of one thing we can be sure. There is order in the universe. If there were no order we could not progress. We could not plan nor could we reach our goals. The very cellular structure of our body would disassemble. If there were no order there would be no universe.

Order is reflected on every level of creation. To our minds some things appear more orderly than others. One way of measuring order is to measure activity. We could say the more activity something exhibits, the less order it has. Probably the clearest and the most striking example of this way of measuring order can be found in your own mind. When you are at peace, in a quiet state of mind, all appears right with your world. You are calm, clear-thinking, and more supportive and loving. When you get angry, when your mind is machine-gunning thoughts in all directions, your thinking becomes agitated, scrambled, derisive and unloving. So we can say that peace is more orderly than anger. In actuality, it is we, not the universe, who have decided which is more or less orderly. Looking at it through the transcendent eyes of the universe, both peace and anger are equally orderly. They both have their value.

As a general rule, life, which includes you and me, moves away from pain and toward pleasure. Anger is uncomfortable. Peace is pleasurable. Our natural tendency is to say that peace is good and anger is bad. The next step is to rationalize peace as more orderly, something we want to increase because it is more pleasurable. There's nothing wrong with feeling that peace is better than anger, as long as we realize that, at their core and on the universal level beyond our limited understanding of cause and effect, both peace and anger are equal. The only way to know universal equality and harmony is to directly perceive the stillness which underlies all creation.

Let's apply this line of reasoning to a piece of fruit, let's say a banana. You bring home a firm yellow banana from the local grocery and place it in a bowl on your dining room table. You get distracted for a few days from banana awareness, and when you notice the banana again it has attracted a small swarm of fruit flies, the skin is covered in black spots, and the meat is mushy. Now, unless you like discolored, fly-fouled, and mushy banana meat you will gingerly pinch the stem of the banana between thumb and forefinger and usher it directly to the garbage, leaving the fruit flies to fend for themselves.

According to Newton's second law of thermodynamics, the original firm banana exhibited greater order than the decomposing one. Remember that is the law which tells us that all energy and matter in the universe are deteriorating (entropy), moving toward a state of inert uniformity. In other words, everything in the universe is deconstructing, falling apart … dying. Boy, talk about your Gloomy Gus. Newton, who was prone to depression anyway, must've had an unusually significant disagreement with his girlfriend the day he thought that one up. But thankfully that is only part of the picture.

Stuff has to decompose so that other stuff can take its place. That is the way of the world, isn't it? Imagine what a fix we would be in if people didn't die. We would either overrun our planet with the undying masses or we would create a stagnant population of a chosen few leaving no room for newcomers. Decomposition or entropy is only part of the picture. Yes, you have the destructive force, but you also have the creative force, don't you? Both are working everywhere all the time. At one time in the banana's life it was growing and then it began to rot. Where is that banana years later? Of course it has been broken down into the molecules, atoms, and subatomic particles from which it was made. Those particles dispersed and reassembled and may now be scattered throughout the universe. Intriguing, isn't it, to think that you may have subatomic particles of banana mush zinging around inside your brain at this very moment? Why, I have known people who couldn't even think that one through because their brains had already turned to banana mush. But that is another story and, again, I digress.

So we have a destructive force and a creative force, and both are absolutely necessary for life to continue. The flower falls from the tree so the fruit may form. The fruit falls from the tree so that the seed may be planted. The seed dies with the birth of the tree and so the cycle repeats itself.

So is that it? Two forces of creation? You might think that is all we need, but upon closer inspection you will see that something is missing. What keeps the two forces together? What keeps them in check? What keeps them from going on and on without end?

Let's focus in on that specific point where creation stops and destruction starts. If you were to take a magnifying glass and zoom in on the creative process just before it turns destructive, what would you find? That's right, stillness! At some point the creative force must stop working before the destructive force can begin. It is exactly at that juncture that you find absolute stillness. Remember when the wave stops going up, and just before it goes down it comes to a complete stop? From your own personal experience, remember what it was like to swing on a swing. Remember how it felt at that exact moment when hanging motionless in mid-air? How about when you did the Nothing Technique? You found stillness, like a motionless movie screen, beyond and between your thoughts, didn't you? The thing is, once you reduce activity to its most basic level, there is no activity, no creation and destruction. Once you take your magnifying glass and keep going into deeper and deeper levels of activity you find stillness waiting for you. It is as if activity is an illusion.

Aware in EuStillness, you break the illusion of unending activity. Or more accurately you see the reality of stillness at the same time you observe the play and display of creative and destructive forces. This creates a sense of permanence, a sense of psychological security because of your direct contact with stillness.

Think about it. What does stillness mean to you? To the activity-oriented mind, stillness has no value – that is, until it realizes that the perception of stillness is the perception of immortality. When your attention is always on activity, then it learns a very depressing lesson. It comes to realize that everything is always changing. If everything is always changing, then ultimately you cannot rely on anything. In the language of Isaac Newton, entropy rules, everything is dying. When your attention is always on activity, all it knows is death.

What in your life has not changed? How about your first love? Do you still love that person the same way today? How do you feel about your job today as compared to the first day you showed up for work? What about your body? Have there been any changes there? How about your beliefs, your fears, your ambitions, and your hopes for the future? Sooner or later, the river of time washes everything beyond our grasp. In the end, the bodies and minds that we are so attached to will die.

Are you feeling a little depressed right now? I just gave you a pretty accurate depiction of life as most people know it. Imagine how hard it is for those of us who are looking to the future to convince ourselves that it holds promise. When we look at it closely, it appears to hold only the promise of death. That is why most of us do not dwell on it. In fact, quite the opposite – Americans especially spend huge amounts of time and energy dedicating their lives to denying death. The beautiful thing is, we don't have to.

So what can we do about it? Well, I think you already know where I'm going. If your life is overwhelmed with activity, then balance it with EuStillness. EuStillness has no beginning or end. It was never created like a molecule, a mountain, or an emotion is created. It has no form. If it has no form, then it cannot decompose. It is beyond the touch of entropy. It is endless and undying. It is EuStillness.

Awareness of EuStillness is awareness of absolute, non-moving, undying stillness at the same time as you are aware of the always-changing, always-moving realm of phenomenal existence. When you do the EuStillness Technique you end up perceiving both at the same time, and this realization has a most remarkable effect on how you live your life. The result is a non-reliance on activity as a way to make you fulfilled. You don't have to make more money, own a bigger home, or impress your friends and their friends by doing whatever you think will impress them. Activity is only half of the game. When you see the stillness within activity, you immediately lose the fear of death. Free of the fear of death, you become less guarded, more relaxed, more naturally who you were meant to be. You become fulfilled, with an inner contentment that lets you enjoy who you are, where you are. You know you are already complete, so you lose the frantic drive to be someone else, somewhere else.

You might now be worried that when you are aware of EuStillness you might become like Uug-lug and sit around all day contemplating your navel. Not so. Aware of EuStillness, you will actually become more motivated, more creative, as well as more energetic, well directed, loving, and fun loving. EuStillness completes life. Do it now ...

- Close your eyes and let your mind wander wherever it wants to go.

- Easily become aware of your thoughts and then look beyond them to find the nothing of pure awareness.

- Become aware of Eufeeling, some sense of well-being, quietness, lightness, etc.

- Look intently into Eufeeling and you will find EuStillness.

- Do the Coin Technique, bringing awareness to the negative and positive in EuStillness.

- Enjoy EuStillness with eyes closed for as long as you like, then open your eyes and do the Stop-Hand technique.

- Simply observe EuStillness wherever you find it.

- Again, become aware of Eufeeling ...

You are ushering yourself into the world of the enlightened transcender, what it means to be fully human. It is the beginning point of balanced living between the polarities of life, young and old, rich and poor, good and bad, dynamic activity and absolute stillness. If not already, soon EuStillness will be there immediately whenever you choose to perceive it. Uniting your life with that area long denied, you will transcend disharmony while in the face of it, overcome adversity while in the midst of it, and safely navigate the rocks of relativity on the sea of stillness. What a wonderful, wonderful journey you are.

Main Points – Chapter 11

- Without awareness we have nothing.

- Awareness and perception change with each state of human consciousness.

- The six major states of awareness are waking, dreaming, deep sleep, pure awareness, EuAwareness, and EuStillness awareness.

- Pure awareness is essential for our spiritual well-being.

- EuAwareness brings the harmonizing influence of pure awareness into daily activity. It is the beginning stage of enlightenment.

- EuStillness is the direct perception of the absolute stillness that is present in everyday activity and objects. It is a necessary step to becoming fully human.

CHAPTER 12

HOW TO MAKE A DECISION OR HOW TO OUT-THINK YOUR GOLDFISH

"Education is not the filling of a pail,
but the lighting of a fire."

~WILLIAM BUTLER YEATS

I want to take a moment with you and play a little bit. My favorite subject in grade school was recess. In fact, as you may well have guessed by now it is *still* my favorite subject. So in the spirit of recess let's take a little break from philosophical pursuits and learn how to make a decision. For many people, especially those overwhelmed by all the choices that we have in industrialized nations, it becomes exceedingly hard to make a decision based on what we know is best for us.

By now we should have a pretty good idea about how damaging too much activity can be. Awareness of activity alone without EuStillness to balance it is the basic cause of discord and suffering in our lives. One form of over-activity is having too many choices to make. The "more is better" mentality is hard at work in the U.S. and other industrialized nations. When I first began driving in my teens, my father only had a few choices to make when he wanted to buy a new car. There were only six or seven car manufacturers, each with a limited line of models to offer in only two or three colors. The other day I decided to look for a new car and I couldn't keep count of all the car manufacturers, much less the models they offered, the colors, the option packages, and incentives. I wanted to walk across the street and buy a bicycle. Then I looked at all the bikes lined up out in front of the cycling shop and said, "Forget it, I'll just walk!" And I did walk, right into a shoe store where I had my choice of somewhere in the neighborhood of 437 different walking shoes. I put my head in my hands and began to weep. But that's not the end of the story. After the EMTs deposited me at my friendly neighborhood mental institution, I was sitting quietly on my hard bed surrounded by my four padded walls with not a single choice to make when the orderly wheeled in a rolling closet and asked me to choose, from a number of styles, sizes and colors, with the option of a personalized monogram, with or without rhinestones, my very own straitjacket. OK, OK, I admit it wasn't that bad, but the point is, having too many choices can be most unsettling and even unhealthy. Science agrees. There are numerous studies demonstrating that while it might be an appealing theory in practice, having too many choices can actually be debilitating.

As we are offered more and more choices, our attention span is actually diminishing. It seems that we need to be entertained or we just lose interest. According to the U.S. National Library of Medicine, in the year 2000 the average American's attention span was 12 seconds. In 2013 it dropped to 8 seconds. That's a 33.3 % decrease in attention span in just 13 years, which to me is abysmal. But wait, you haven't heard the most unsettling statistic. The average attention span of a goldfish is 9 seconds, one second longer than the average American! An employer looking over the newest crop of prospective employees had best choose the ones with gills.

When our attention is being pulled in so many different directions it makes it almost impossible to make a healthy decision. An article published on March 7, 2014 in *Neuroscience* magazine cited a study done by Columbia University Medical Center. Researchers there found that decision-making accuracy can be improved: "Postponing the onset of the decision process by as little as 50 to 100 milliseconds enables the brain to *focus attention* [my italics] on the most relevant information and block out irrelevant distractors ..." said author Jack Grinband. Here's the part that interested me: the article stated that the mechanism that enables the decision-maker to improve decision-making accuracy is to "do nothing". Does that sound at all familiar? Of course it does, as you already know the value of nothing. It looks like science is just now catching up to you.

You also know that doing nothing is what happens when you become aware of EuStillness. After all, that's what stillness is, isn't it? If just a pause of as little as 50 to 100 milliseconds can improve your decision-making, what do you think will happen when you take 5 minutes to dive headfirst into EuStillness? Let's find out, shall we?

The EuStillness Decision Technique

- Become aware of EuStillness (1 to 2 minutes).

- Become aware of the situation and the decision you have to make.

- Become aware of all of your possible choices, one at a time.

- With each new possible choice, become aware of how you feel. Is the feeling negative (creates confusion, anxiety, or some other adverse reaction) or positive (creates a sense of relief, clarity, or some other supportive reaction)?

- Become easily aware of the most positive solution.

- Return to EuStillness (1 minute).

- Look into EuStillness to see if any new solutions surface. If no new solutions arise, then sit in EuStillness, occasionally thinking about the most positive solution and then letting your mind wander for 15 to 30 seconds. Then repeat several more times, returning to EuStillness, your most positive solution, and then letting your mind wander.

- Become aware of Eufeeling and gently end this session.

The EuStillness Decision Technique works like a charm for quieting and organizing your mind and gently alerting you to the derisive forces underlying making a decision. Simultaneously, it quickly quells anxiety and the other emotions that interfere with decision-making.

Interestingly and as an aside, you might find the solutions to other problems you have might suddenly appear fully wrapped and ready to open like an early birthday present.

When do you know you are done making a decision? You know you have the right decision when you feel completely comfortable with it. You have a kind of "knowing", a clear intuition that it is real and right. There is no doubt.

If there is doubt about your decision, then do the EuStillness Decision Technique again the following day, and the next day if necessary. This is usually only necessary when there is a great deal of emotional trauma attached to making your decision. But the need for this is rare. Don't be in a hurry. That only slows things down. Don't look for results but take the results you get. If the results are inconclusive, then wait a bit and repeat the EuStillness Decision Technique. Remember, the idea is to do nothing, right? So don't try to help out or hurry up the process. That is the fastest and easiest way to get your answer.

Trying to find an answer, actively looking for it, will push the answer away. It's kind of like this: Let's say we are sitting at the edge of a clear pool. Then when I tell you that you can see the answer at the bottom of the pool, you begin splashing away the surface water so that you can see what is on the bottom. Obviously, moving the surface water only creates distortions and prevents you from seeing clearly what is on the bottom. Actively looking for an answer during the EuStillness Decision Technique is like disturbing the waters. It is the still mind which sees clearly.

Almost always you have a clear course of action by the end of the session. In fact you may find that halfway through your session, or even during the preparatory first minute of EuStillness, the answer will pop into your mind along with a knowing smile on your face. As you practice

The EuStillness Decision Technique you will be able to do it in the blink of an eye, even without taking time to sit down or even close your eyes.

OK, time to move on to our next chapter. Ready to fall in love?

Main Points – Chapter 12

- Having too many choices can actually be debilitating.

- Even as we are offered more choices, our attention span is diminishing.

- Researchers found that experiencing "nothing" for as little as 50 to 100 milliseconds can improve the accuracy of decision-making.

- The EuStillness Decision Technique works like a charm for quieting and organizing your mind and gently alerting you to the derisive forces underlying making a decision.

- You know you have the right decision when you feel completely comfortable with it, a kind of "knowing", a clear intuition that it is real and right. There is no doubt.

- When you do the EuStillness Decision Technique you almost always receive a clear course of action.

CHAPTER 13

MAKING LOVE

"A loving heart is the beginning of all knowledge."
~Thomas Carlyle

Aahhh, love: birds singing, bees buzzing, and hearts all aflutter. That's what most often comes to mind when we first hear that most titillating of words isn't it? ... Two souls, passions inflamed, hearts and limbs entwined, head over heels in ... romantic love. But there is more to love than this notorious but much sought-after, quixotic, if not quick, episode of unbridled euphoria; much more.

If I asked you to name other expressions of love, you might mention the brotherly love of family, friends, and community, or parental love, the love of a mother for her child, or the mature love of one spouse for another. You might remind me that there is the cleaner love of beauty and of knowledge and the love of a single soul for that ultimate One, God. But these are all forms of love appreciated from the human perspective. What of rock love or atomic love or universal love? Does such a thing exist? And if so, what is it and what impact might it have on your life? I'd like to introduce you to a visionary paradigm of love that will momentously impact your life, immediately and forever. I am talking about a unique and universal love, the one love from which all other expressions of love emanate.

I am not talking about an abstract theory here. I wouldn't waste your time with that. Nor am I recommending that you "learn" to love by practicing forgiveness, charity, acceptance, serenity, or the like. These reflections of human harmony do not need to be practiced, for they will spontaneously radiate from you when you know how a mountain or a molecule loves.

I guess the first order of the day would be to define love. Now don't get all gushy on me here. Of course the first thing we think about when we hear the word "love" is an emotional bond between two people. Love is that, but it is so much more. I know, the poets and the songwriters can't do it, so what makes me think that I can define love? Well, first let me take a stab at defining universal love, and then guide you to your own inner experience of that most precious perception.

Now this definition of love is a pretty lengthy and in-depth one, so make sure you have your thinking caps pulled down firmly on your heads. Here is my definition of love: *when two things unite to create greater harmony.* OK, so my definition is a little shorter than most, but it is very functional. Let's find out how.

Obviously when two people unite in love (I will let your imagination dictate what is meant by "unite" here), greater harmony is enjoyed between them. But can two atoms love? It would seem, at least by my definition, two atoms can make love. When two atoms unite to create the greater harmony of a molecule, that is love. The mating of molecules to create stars, cars, and candy bars is an overt expression of love that can't be denied. (Especially the candy bar part.) The creative process and all that it produces is the expression of universal love. And how do I define universal love? Universal love is: *the force that unites.* If we call the force that unites love, then what do we call the force that tears creation apart? The classical physicist would call it *entropy* and the Eastern philosopher would call it *tamas.* Pardon my flair for the dramatic, but I often use the word "death". Since we have previously discussed at length negativity and death, I don't think we need to dwell on it further. I bring it up now only to place it in context with love.

I think I did a pretty good job defining love, at least in practical terms, but the definition doesn't get you any closer to actually knowing what love is, does it? Well, guess what? Once you know how, the force of universal love is easier to *experience* than it is to define. In fact, if you have been doing your EuStillness homework, then you are 90% of the way there. Let's find out what I mean.

Awareness of EuStillness is awareness of pure awareness while you are thinking and while you are actively going about your day. It is the direct perception of absolute stillness in objects and activities. When you learned the EuStillness Technique you entered into that stillness through Eufeeling. Eufeeling comes from EuStillness. Some will say that pure awareness is love. But pure awareness is not a force. It has no form or energy. It just is. The child of pure awareness is EuStillness. EuStillness is unexpressed universal love. The child of EuStillness is Eufeeling, the first expression of universal love. The children of expressed universal love, or Eufeeling, are every created thing. When I use the term "universal love" it can mean either EuStillness or Eufeeling depending on the context. Both are universal. EuStillness is unexpressed universal love, and Eufeeling is the first and only expression of love that is universal.

The hierarchy looks like this:

EuStillness → Eufeeling → Every created thing

When pure light strikes a prism, it creates a rainbow of seven colors. When the pure light enters the prism it goes through a transition, a kind of bending or stirring before it breaks up into red, orange, yellow, green, blue, indigo, and violet. When those colors mix they produce the infinite array of color hues we see everywhere around us. EuStillness is like the pure light. When EuStillness strikes the prism, stillness begins to stir into existence. This stirring of stillness is the birth of Eufeeling. The reflections of Eufeeling like peace, joy, contentment, bliss, awe, compassion, etc. are analogous to the colors that radiate from the prism. Those initial reflections of Eufeeling go on to produce things and thoughts throughout the universe. So you could correctly say that the biscotti you dunked into your cup of coffee this morning is actually Eufeeling being dunked into Eufeeling.

Remember in the last chapter when you learned how to make a decision? In actuality you did not consciously make the decision, isn't that right? The realization of "rightness" was spontaneous. When you recognized the right course of action you just "knew" it was right, right? That was your intuition kicking in. Your next question should be, "What is intuition?" Well, I am so glad you asked, because I prepared an answer and it would be a shame if you had never inquired.

Intuition is the quietest, subtlest, most refined reflection of Eufeeling. Intuition is actually two entities in seed form. You know them in your mind as thinking and feeling. Remember how everything in creation has both form and energy? In regards to intuition, thinking would be analogous to form and feeling to energy. Thinking includes thought processes like logic, analysis, reasoning, and synthesis. Thinking processes are not creative. They are convergent, looking more closely at and defining what already exists. Feeling (and for the sake of simplicity I use feeling and emotion interchangeably) is the opposite of thinking. It is abstract and expansive. Feeling, which also includes imagination, has the power to sweep us away to worlds unknown.

Einstein once said that imagination is more important than knowledge. I don't agree with this statement, and here is the reason why. In a healthy mind, thinking and feeling work together. They are like a train and the tracks. Your thinking tracks are well ordered, well-defined, and move in a specific direction toward your destination. Your emotion train provides the power and the drive to get you to that destination. Without the tracks the train would chug around in circles trying to find direction. Without the train the tracks have no purpose. Whether you are a scientist or a songwriter, the creative process is the same. The problem is to get from where you are to your destination. Feeling is first. In the form of desire, feeling motivates you to move, then thinking provides the tools and the direction for fulfillment. If Einstein meant that imagination was more important because it comes first, then I can climb back on board the Einstein train and choo-choo off to the stars at the speed of light.

Intuition is the first child of Eufeeling, the first form of love that is not universal. Intuition holds within her womb the twins, thinking and feeling. Upon their birth they traverse their separate paths. But before their birth, snuggled in the womb of intuition there is no distance between them. As with all twins, no matter how far they range afield, they will always share their extraordinary bond of intimacy. They are as one, two sides of the same coin.

When you become aware of intuition, as you did in the EuStillness Decision Technique, you become aware of her children, thinking and feeling, before they separate. This is what makes intuition so special. This is how, in a flash of insight, you get the answer to your problem. Along with the feeling that the answer is absolutely right comes the simultaneous thinking of how to go about reaching the solution. When you have a clear perception of intuition, your thinking and feeling are working in perfect harmony. That means you are one with the oneness which buys you a front row seat to creation, in this case the play and display of thinking and feeling.

If you do a survey of us humans you'll see that we are loosely divided into the two camps, the thinkers and the feelers. Now I know this is a very general classification, but bear with me a moment longer and you will see the point I make has validity. As soon as thinking and feeling take form, so does the entire field of opposites, especially negativity and positivity. Let's consider the traditional classical scientist who thinks that she is an objective observer and that science is a reflection of that objectivity. She thinks the artist, who revels in the world of abstraction, is illogical and undisciplined. The artist feels quite comfortable without boundaries and he views the scientist's life as stilted and dry. Now here's the point: commonly each inwardly feels and thinks that their approach is better than the others, don't they? The scientist, who does not understand how the artist can have such unstructured thinking, feels more comfortable living with laws and formulas and data. If you forced an artist into those confines you would sentence him to death by boredom. Neither the artist nor the scientist can appreciate the other's point of view and so they remain divided, resistant, and closed to compromise.

Neither realizes that they are themselves incomplete without the mastery of both.

These negative and non-compliant attitudes are weeds in the garden of love. They are germinated in the rocky soil of Maslow's lower needs. When you are aware of EuStillness you are a living, breathing transcender. You have made friends with intuition; you move easily through this garden of perfect imperfection. And like any master gardener you know that weeds are a part of life. Your acceptance is not born of any superficial philosophy (thinking) or contrived imagery (feeling). You do not need to try to culture love. You perceive the womb of intuition where the twins of thinking and feeling are united, and therefore appreciate the expressions of both on every level of life. You have no need to hold one higher than the other. Settled in EuStillness, you are a quiet observer to the unfoldment of their respective energies within your mind. Aware of all permeating oneness, you are free of the influence of opposites.

When EuStill, when you perceive stillness as the single commonality to all things, you know opposites as you did before and you still have your individual preferences. However, on the deepest level you appreciate the value of both – and therein lies the difference. You don't have to defend one point of view or discredit the other. You may choose to, momentarily, but ultimately you perceive your existence as beyond opposites. As we discussed earlier, this is how the transcender ultimately views all opposites, with acceptance and equanimity. This acceptance allows you to appreciate the genius of creation, which sharpens your perception, which likewise deepens your appreciation, all the while planting more firmly in your awareness the subtle profundity of universal love.

We just spent a few pages delving into the mechanics of universal love, definitely an exercise skewed towards the thinking mind. But the really, really neat thing about universal love is that you don't have to understand it to live it. In actuality, we can never understand the universal side of universal love. But we can wallow in its richness and celebrate its reflection in even the most mundane expressions of life. How? Why, you already know the answer, don't you? Become aware of EuStillness and then play, play, play!

And in the spirit of play, here is a simple experience to bring you in closer alignment with the expressions of thinking and feeling in your mind.

The EuStillness Universal (Unbounded) Love Experience

- Become aware of EuStillness (1 to 2 minutes).

- Remember a time when you felt unbounded love (either from you or to you).

- Become aware of the thoughts around your love.

- Become aware of the feeling behind the thoughts.

- Again, become aware of your unbounded love.

- Again, become aware of your thoughts and feelings and note how your unbounded love is in your thoughts and feelings – they both come from unbounded love, are made from, and are full of unbounded love.

- Become easily and clearly aware of unbounded love. Look into it to see what is inside. There you will find absolute stillness, EuStillness.

- Become aware of EuStillness (30 seconds).

- Become aware of Eufeeling …

Nothing feels better than to be confident about where you are headed. That confidence adds deeply to the quality of your life. It is one of the greater joys of becoming fully human. Now it is time for us to turn our attention outward to embrace the relationships we have with those souls who inhabit this big blue marble with us. Now is the time for us to go beyond ourselves and, as a species, evolve into universal love. The first step of that journey is to find out where we are. From there we must learn the new laws that will govern our transformation. And to do that we will begin with a singularly profound insight from an anthropologist turned systems scientist. He discovered a simple, irrefutable truth that when ignored leads to the death of the system. What was this astonishing discovery and can we apply it to our own lives?

Well, what are you waiting for? Turn the page!

Main Points – Chapter 13

- Love: *when two things unite to create greater harmony.*

- Universal love: *the force that unites.*

- Universal love cannot be learned by practicing forgiveness, charity, acceptance, serenity, or the like. Universal love can only be lived through direct experience.

- EuStillness is unexpressed universal love. Eufeeling is expressed universal love. Eufeeling is the child of EuStillness.

- Intuition is the quietest, subtlest, most refined reflection of Eufeeling.

- Thinking and feeling are born in the womb of intuition.

- The "thinkers" and the "feelers" of the world find common ground in EuStillness, both between each other and within themselves.

CHAPTER 14

THE THEORY OF
TRANSFORMATION:

Evolving into Universal Love

"The extraordinary thing about nature is that all success leads to failure: repeating success is an inevitable way to guarantee failure!"

~GEORGE LAND, DISCOVERER
OF THE THEORY OF TRANSFORMATION

It was a blindingly hot day in June, 2013. The car's air-conditioning fought valiantly against the 109°F (43°C) heat monster clawing for purchase just a quarter-inch away on the other side of my car window. It was as if the heat was trying to run away from itself and find refuge inside with me. But my artificially created and increasingly precarious inner car ecology was lukewarm and losing. Heat was no friend of mine that day.

You might well ask, "What possible motive could you have that would take you into the Arizona desert in the midst of summer?" I was on my way to meet a scientist. To be more specific, I would soon be in the company of, assuming my tires didn't melt into the pavement, George Ainsworth Land, a systems scientist and the discoverer of the theory of transformation. According to my rental car's navigational system I was 3.4 miles from the home of Dr. Land and I began to feel a thread of excitement tugging at some unknown entity deep within my psyche. I had been introduced to Dr. Land's work some 15 years earlier and it had inspired in me a reorganization, as it were, of basic tenets upon which I formerly lived and taught. Because of the theory of transformation I began to see organization in a world that was previously chaotic. I'll share more of this with you in a moment, but first back inside the rental car.

I made a quick right turn and rolled into the driveway of Dr. Land's home. I took a few seconds to compose myself. Dr. Land was in his mid-eighties and I expected a somewhat frail, slightly bent man with possibly a light shuffle. I reminded myself to speak more loudly and slowly to make myself heard and understood. I knocked firmly on the door and waited.

I was startled when the door flew open. I looked up, and then up some more at a tall, robust frame with well-developed arms that were reaching out for me. I might have turned and ran had I not looked into his eyes: clear, blue, and kind, unveiling a knowing glint. Atop his eyes ambled two furry white caterpillar eyebrows. His suntanned face was framed by a snow white beard that merged with snow white hair, creating the illusion that his face was floating in the clouds.

His voice, deep and resident, rumbled like soft thunder, "So good to finally meet you, Frank," he said. As we hugged his powerful arms completely engulfed me, banishing any thoughts of frailty. A few minutes later we were comfortably situated in Land's living room, papers and books spread on the round, mosaic coffee table between us. I spent all that day and most of the next asking Land questions, posing alternate and hypothetical scenarios, but mostly bathing in the fountain of wisdom that flowed from the mind of this keenest of observers of the hidden lessons of life. Here is what he told me ...

The theory of transformation is a way to understand how Nature grows and evolves in perfect harmony. Nature does exactly what it should, when it should. (Just this realization alone has brought peace and harmony to many souls searching for some semblance of order and purpose in their world.) Nature is more than reactive; it is creative. Furthermore, it exhibits three distinct levels of creativity, three unique phases of growth and change. Everything in Nature from an atom to a galaxy, from a business to a bumblebee, traverses these three phases of growth and transformation. Once you understand how these levels interact you have a roadmap that tells you exactly where you have come from, where you are presently, and where you are going. Knowing what Nature expects from you helps you avoid the potholes and dead ends that bewilder and befuddle the uninformed traveler. It gives you the greatest chance for a productive, successful, and happy life.

Land wrote in his book, *Breakpoint and Beyond: Mastering the Future Today,* co-authored with his wife and soulmate Beth Jarman, "I researched biology, genetics, chemistry, anthropology, psychology, cosmology, and atomic physics. In *every* case, I found the same essential natural process of creativity operating. What was even more significant is that this knowledge changed my life radically. It provided me with a context to understand how everything fits together and works. Suddenly what had seemed so disorderly and chaotic in my world made sense. It revealed how I could successfully deal with great changes in my own life and assist the organizations I worked with in applying the simple laws of Nature."

(Note: Land calls the three phases of transformation *forming, norming,* and *fulfilling.* Forgive me, George, but because it better serves our purpose here I am going to take poetic license and instead will substitute the terms *survival, expansion,* and *love* to represent phases 1, 2, and 3, respectively.) Each phase is dependent on the successful completion of the previous one. You cannot skip from survival to love. Nature will have none of that. Each phase also has its own unique laws that must be followed if success is to be realized. As you will see, breaking these laws means certain failure. I have often heard people remark that Nature is cruel. Nature only appears to be cruel when you don't understand the laws that underlie an event. Cruelty is a human invention. A wildfire ravaging thousands of square acres of forest may be thought of as cruel or wasteful until you understand that the benefits of a forest fire – killing invasive weeds and eradicating plant diseases, cleaning the forest floor, opening it to light and water, and enriching forest nutrition among others – is a natural part of the cycle of a healthy forest. Nature does not make mistakes. It takes a self-serving human mind to label the natural creative process a mistake. So let's take this chance to un-muddle our minds and in so doing realize what a remarkable natural phenomenon we are.

Let's start by taking a closer look at each phase of the theory of transformation. Survival or phase 1, is characterized by invention, a dynamic exploration to find patterns and processes that will connect the organism with its environment. The creative energy of expansion, or phase 2, is focused on building on what works. Growth in this phase comes from repeating what works, improving on it, and then extending it. Love, or phase 3, is characterized by innovation, creating something completely new and different by including elements that were rejected in phase 1. In a moment I will explain these three phases and show you everyday examples that illustrate how they work in Nature and relationships. Simply put, a grasp of these simple principles and knowing how to put them into action can fully transform your life.

The Three Phases of the Theory of Transformation

- Phase 1 – Survival: The stage of growth where the type of creativity relies on invention. The growing organism is searching for an initial pattern of successful growth that will connect with its environment.

- Phase 2 – Expansion: Once a first phase pattern has been invented, growth demands that creativity shifts to building on a pattern, by repeating, improving, and extending it.

- Phase 3 – Love: A system opens to creative innovation. This requires unifying and integrating what was previously excluded, and including the new and the different within the old pattern.

Land defines a system as a collection of parts that make up something that is unified and whole. The reason this definition is important is that the three phases of creative transformation are operating in every system. Organically, a system could be an individual, a single cell, the history of cell evolution, an organization, or an entire culture. It can also be a molecule, a mountain, a Maserati, or our living, breathing Earth. Let's now take time to reveal the heart and the soul of the theory of transformation.

Let's first follow the lifecycle of an acorn. The acorn falls from the tree, is buried in the soil, and awaits germination. As soon as the acorn germinates it goes into its survival mode. It has to quickly assess its environment in order to sprout and grow. One of the first things the sprouting acorn must do is determine which way is up. It also has to begin taking in the proper amount of moisture and food, and to excrete its toxins. If anything is less than optimal, for instance the soil is too acidic, the seed must adapt quickly to continue sprouting. In the survival phase the sprout must assimilate what is beneficial and eliminate what is not.

If all goes right the sprout stabilizes its growth and becomes a sapling. The sapling's job is to eventually grow into a mature oak tree. To get there it already knows what to do, repeat what is successful, improve on it, and then extend. Those are the main attributes of phase 2, the expansion phase. Now it is all about the sapling growing into the tree. The sapling, like any child, takes everything it needs from its environment and invests it in growing stronger and taller. The sapling's surroundings provide everything it needs but get little back in return.

When the sapling finally becomes a tree it begins to give back to its environment. This is a major characteristic of phase 3, the love phase. Remember, love is when two things unite to create greater harmony. The environment continues to sustain the tree, but now the oak tree is able to give back. The mature oak tree cleans the air, combating greenhouse gases, and produces oxygen. It transpires moisture into the atmosphere, reduces water pollution and soil erosion, fertilizes the soil, provides food for wildlife and humans, provides a protective canopy for wildlife, and produces little acorns so the cycle may continue. In essence everything benefits from this synergistic love relationship between the oak tree and its surroundings.

It would be good to note here that the attributes of all three phases can be found in any single phase at any time, but the distinguishing attributes of any one phase will be dominant. For instance, the expansion phase is characterized by finding what works and then improving and increasing that. But the expansion phase will also entertain periods of phase 1 surviving and inventing or the phase 3 use of previously discarded ideas and experiences to reinvent itself. But there can be only one primary and driving force in each phase. Obviously in each phase of the oak's growth you can observe flavors of the other phases, but they do not dominate that phase.

While this is all well and good for an oak tree and its environs, what about a relationship between two people? Let's look in on John and Marsha as they progress through the three phases of their romantic relationship as it unfolds into universal love. Let's follow them as they meet and fall in romantic love, stabilize and grow within their commitment, reach a crisis point at the end of phase 2, and finally grow into the transformational love phase where they will create a completely new relationship.

John snatched the last outside table at a crowded coffee shop. He was lazily scrolling through his emails on his smartphone while sipping lazily on a large skinny soy latte minus whip plus sprinkles when he looked up and saw her. She was standing in a splash of sunlight as if descended from heaven. She was looking for a seat and, without a thought John stood, arm extended palm up indicating the open seat at his table. Marsha noticed him for the first time and her face brightened. Her feet began moving before her mind realized that she had accepted his invitation. After a few minutes of stilted small talk they fell into the flow of familiarity. They were brand new to each other but it felt as if they were old friends. When he heard the telling slurp from her empty cup, John chivalrously offered to buy Marsha another.

"What are you drinking?" he asked.

"A large skinny soy latte minus whip plus sprinkles" she answered, and at that instant John knew he had just met his lifelong soulmate right there. Phase one of their relationship was off to a roaring start.

Over the next few months John and Marsha spent every available moment with each other. They went to concerts and movies, went biking and hiking, took tango lessons and danced the night away. They had long serious talks sharing their beliefs, their hopes, and fears, inviting each other deeply into their lives and their souls. They laughed, they loved, and they experimented testing the boundaries of their burgeoning bonds. They introduced each other to new ideas, emotions, and experiences, and together explored each with a passion that only fresh love can create.

Not everything worked. They visited an abstract art gallery that titillated Marsha but had John hiding ever-widening yawns behind the back of his hand. He took her to a hockey game. While John stood through most of the game cheering and yelling and shaking his fist, Marsha alternately covered her ears and her eyes as she recoiled from the noise and violence. What didn't work was casually left by the roadside as they journeyed onward ever seeking out new experiences to share with each other.

As their fondness for each other grew they began the second phase of their relationship, repeating, improving, and expanding on what was working. They found an inexpensive apartment in town, moved in together, and settled into a routine. They looked at their union as the beginning of a lifelong promise of mutual growth and support. It became less spontaneous and more predictable. They relinquished their all-night talks in favor of a good night's sleep. They substituted a weekend at a seaside resort with a walk in the park to save money for a complete home theater system. They got more responsible jobs that came with more responsible friends. As if to practice for greater things to come, they adopted an 8-week-old golden Labrador Retriever and named her Lady. After six months of cohabitation John bent a knee and popped the question. Marsha answered, "Yes, I will marry you!" and one year later to the day they consecrated their lifelong commitment in holy matrimony.

For those first seven years the light of their union illuminated substantial and even wondrous joys. They brought two beautiful children into the world, a rambunctious boy (John Jr.) and a bright and curious girl (Alexandra). They both got promotions at work while Marsha attended night school toward a Master of Business Administration degree. They bought a home in a well-manicured suburb boasting a good school system. John and Marsha were proud of their lives and were enthusiastic and hopeful for their future.

During the next seven years the bloom began to lose its luster. That period consumed most of John and Marsha's third decade of life. The energy and enthusiasm of their 20s gave way to the shoulder-to-the-grindstone, dogged determination of their 30s. Their children, their jobs, and financial stress consumed their energies, leaving very little quality time for each other.

In their early 40s both John and Marsha secretly felt that something was missing from their marriage. With all the responsibilities they had incurred toward reaching their goal of a happy, functional family, they actually spent very little time together. Where once their lives revolved around each other they now splintered their time against the myriad family necessities such as work, getting the kids to appointments, grocery shopping, social functions, church activities, household repairs, paying the bills, and so on and so forth. They found almost no time for lazy conversation, the kind where they caught up on the day's happenings, shared opinions on current events, gossiped about neighbors and family, and opened up to dreams of things to come. Upon returning from their yearly vacation, originally designed to rejuvenate and inject a sense of fun and adventure into their existence, they were more exhausted than before they left. Sex became infrequent and short lived, more an act of physical release, lacking the original passion that demanded time and tenderness. Pillow talk, once robust and inspired, faded quickly into the blessed oblivion of sleep.

The deep inner dissatisfaction each carried within them began to be expressed outwardly. They began to bicker and snipe at each other. They met people at work and in social occasions who reflected the freedom and fun they once had with each other. They began to wonder what it would be like with a different partner. They felt horribly isolated. George Washington once said, "It's better to be alone than in bad company." He believed that it is better to remove yourself from a relationship than to stay with one that doesn't work. At the end of many phase 2 relationships couples feel such ill-will towards each other that, while continuing to live together they emotionally isolate themselves, living out the rest of their lives in self-imposed seclusion. The couple can't return to the exuberance they felt in phase 1, or the sense of accomplishment in phase 2, and they haven't found the key to open themselves to the universal love awaiting them in phase 3. They are stuck, and as we know you cannot stay in one place. As Land says, you either grow or die. So they can only watch helplessly as the beauty they once were dwindles and dies.

This is what Land means when he says, "Nothing fails like success." John and Marsha were successful in exploring their relationship in phase 1, making the transition to phase 2, then building and expanding their phase 2 relationship. When they took inventory of their circumstances, John and Marsha had to admit they were living the "good life". They should be overjoyed with all they had achieved. Then why, in moments of quiet reflection, did they feel so isolated, so dissatisfied with each other and life in general? What neither realized is that it was time to move on, not to a new partner or another life but to the next transformative phase. What the hapless pair did not understand was one of the basic tenets of transformation theory. They're very success changed their environment. The changes created new and different needs for them. Their relatively freewheeling lifestyle of phase 1 gave way to the more stable routine of phase 2. As their needs changed, their environment changed, from which new needs arose.

Let's explore phases 1 and 2 from a slightly different perspective and then discover how EuStillness ties it all together in one neat little package with the ribbon of universal love.

John and Marsha's survival phase was driven by the feeling of romantic love, a foreshadowing of the upcoming universal love of phase 3. The expansion phase depends on the stability of planning and working toward goals. In order to transform their relationship, John and Marsha must first revisit the excitement and exuberance of the first few months of their survival phase. In the waning days of phase 2 they tried to recapture that exuberance by doing the things they used to do. The mistake was this: It was not having breakfast at 5 AM in a diner after sharing their deepest secrets that brought them closer together. It was not the event. It was the sharing of that activity with a kindred soul, someone who was open, vibrant, and creative and who fully supported them that generated their remarkable appetite for life. They were naturally imaginative and creative. But lopsided living is doomed. Their phase 1 lives reflected little order and direction and a great expenditure of energy. Like a shooting star, they risked burning brightly but briefly. To survive they had to transition to the more measured influences of gathering data, planning, and sticking to that plan, in the expansion phase. This John and Marsha did, but at the expense of spontaneity. Phase 3 integrates the spontaneity of phase 1 with the order of phase 2. These are two elements that are united in the love phase.

The couple was also ignorant of a second important precept of the theory of transformation which reveals that a successful system, in this case John and Marsha's relationship, eventually becomes so large and complex that it exhausts its ability to grow. At this point the system has to redefine its relationship with its environment and within itself. It has to come up with a new definition for growth, because the old formula for success no longer works. Nothing fails like success. It was time for John and Marsha to learn the real meaning of love.

Eckert Tolle, often referred to as the most spiritually influential person in the world today, tells us the reason for a relationship is not to fall in love but to become aware. Tolle here refers to conditional love. But what is it that he wants us to become aware of? Tolle advocates awareness of pure awareness as the foundation for universal love. When you become aware of pure awareness you transcend conditional love, recalibrate your love meter for unconditional love, then burst upon the world inspiring health, happiness, and harmony. You not only understand this but you also know how to *be* universal love. Tolle believes that this simple perception can save humankind from self-destruction. So do I.

So you see their dilemma. John and Marsha can neither go back to the innovative feeling of phase 1 nor continue in the fundamental thinking of phase 2. It is the nature of life to grow. The discomfort and disillusionment they are experiencing is evidence that their relationship is entropic, coming apart like an un-lived in house. Mother Nature whispers softly at first and later more loudly, "There is a path beyond despair where joy still lives." They need only listen.

In order to hear Mother Nature you must perceive Her essence. Remarkably, it is your essence too. EuStillness contains in seed form all the instructions needed to live and love. EuStillness is the order that permeates all thoughts and things. When you are unaware of the essence that binds all thoughts and things, you are unable to know how they relate to each other on that most basic level. If you see bricks and cement and wood and wires you can appreciate each individually. What you cannot know is what the master builder will do with those materials. But when he shows you the blueprint you know that they will become a two-bedroom bungalow instead of a fast food franchise.

One of the problems John and Marsha face is that they more than likely will have no idea what a phase 3 love relationship is like, much less how to live that love. After all, how many universally loving couple role models are available these days? If 1% of the population are transcenders, then how much less likely is it that two transcenders would meet, find strong enough common ground to fall in love, and finally grow together into universal love?

Creating Our World View

The following chart is taken from Land and Jarman's *Breakpoint and Beyond*. It compares the difference in perspective between people in the phase 2 and phase 3, expansion and love phases. I thought you would find it most enlightening to see what world view lies behind the behavior of each. Generally speaking, you can align the phase 2 qualities with Maslow's lower needs, and phase 3 with self-actualizers. (Please note: the original chart used "norming" and "fulfillment" which I have changed to "expansion" and "love".)

CHANGING OUR WORLD VIEW	
From Expansion (Phase 2) to Love (Phase 3)	
Thinking Methods	
Logical/rational	Creative/imaginative
Linear/continuous	Nonlinear/discontinuous
Analyzing	Synthesizing/integrating
Knowing	Learning/exploring
Deductive	Inductive
Conscious/calculating	Intuitive
Attitude	
Certain	Curious
Judging	Choices based on vision
Parting with the Past	
Responding/reacting	Initiating/anticipating
Comparing with the past	Experiencing the present
Monotonous	Wonder/awe/enthusiasm
Egoist	Healthy ego
Codependent	Interdependent
Discordant	Harmonious
Cynical	Optimistic
Values	
Fondness	Loving
Guilty	Self-accepting
Pleasure for its own sake	Joy

CHANGING OUR WORLD VIEW *From Expansion (Phase 2) to Love (Phase 3)*	
Secretive/guarded	Open/honest/forthright
Competitive	Cooperative
Problems-centered	Opportunity-centered
Owning/getting	Sharing
Gain/loss	Win/win
Holding on	Letting go
Protective/defensive	Open/visible
Safe/secure	Adventuresome
Beliefs	
Fear/dread/anxiety	Trust/wonder/reverence
Suspicion	Trust
Judging/blame/fault	Acceptance
Scarcity	Abundance
Limits	Potentials
Sexism/racism	Accepting differences
Good/bad/right/wrong	Nonjudgmental
Conservative/traditional	Evolutionary
Repeating old patterns	Exploring new ideas
Protecting the past	Creating the future

There are certainly beautiful examples of long-term loving relationships, but when you ask a couple how they did it they often respond with a platitude or two like, "We never go to bed angry" or "We respect and honor each other." The actual nuts and bolts of the love phase are unknown to them. They truly do not understand how it is they love each other so deeply; they just know they do. That is all about to change. It is now time for us to bring our attention to bear on those very nuts and bolts of universal love.

When you let your awareness dwell in EuStillness, your first perception is that stillness is all-permeating. This perception brings with it a sense of wholeness, fullness, and underlying order. This sense of order and wholeness gives rise to Eufeeling. Eufeeling is the blueprint. Aware of Eu-Stillness and Eufeeling, your perception moves outward to the expressions of intuition and feeling and thinking. These are the bricks and wood and wires of creation. Eu-Stillness is the potential, Eufeeling is the expression, the master builder holding in his mind the completed picture, all of the pieces, and how to bring them all together.

Land speaks often of something he calls future pull. He has called it, "the most powerful force driving change . . . " EuStillness holds that force in the palm of its hand. What is that most powerful force driving change? Why, Eufeeling. When you become aware of EuStillness, Eu-feeling awakens in you, guiding you, pulling you into your future.

Your phase 3 future of universal love will draw from the past, from people, things, and events previously passed over. At the same time you will enter the new world of love, the merging of ideas and people, places and events to create greater and greater harmony. Awareness of Eu-Stillness places you in a unique position. When you have a pure perception of your inner essence you know when something is not right for you. Drop a grain of sand in a glass of dirty water and you will not be able to distinguish it from the other impurities. Drop a grain of sand in a glass of pure water and you can easily pick it out. Your intuition becomes purified, providing perfect perception. You see more opportunities for harmony and make more right decisions. You find yourself smiling and laughing more often. You feel less afraid or anxious or overly cautious. You enjoy others' company but you don't need them to feel complete. You are your own person. You feel a kind of cosmic friendliness towards not only people but things. You recognize that you and a rock share the same stillness. Raindrops tapping on the surface of a puddle can fill you with unexpected joy. Everything is alive with stillness.

For John and Marsha, to become universal lovers they must first let go of their present relationship. They can't possibly build a new one if they are holding on to the old one. Oddly, it reminds me of a monkey swinging from branch to branch. He moves effortlessly through the trees when he lets go of one branch to grasp the next. If he doesn't let go he will dangle forever at the end of a single stick. Silly, I know, but it makes the point.

So what specifically are John and Marsha letting go of? They are letting go of themselves, the pictures in their mind that tells them who they are. This is an outdated album. It's time to put that album on the shelf and begin anew. The new pictures all start from stillness. This is their new reference point, the touchstone of stillness. John and Marsha each must first become friends with their own inner essence. If they do not, every thought, word, and action they perform will be based on one of the lower motivations like guilt from the past or anxiety over the future. This is what I call "future-pasting" which has us jumping from the past to the future and back again in an effort to find out who we are. Who we are can only be found in present, unmoving stillness.

The thing John and Marsha must do to transition to the love phase is for each to discover who they are individually, their inner core or essence. They already know each other superficially. Marsha knows that John doesn't seem to be able to replace the cap back on the toothpaste tube and that he needs to be left alone for a day or two before he is willing to share what is troubling him. John knows that Marsha denies that she snores even when her own snoring wakes her up at night and that she worries about the children leaving home even though that time is still some years away. These personality traits are important to understand for growth and expansion in phase 2, but something much more primal must be understood before they can transcend this relative superficiality. Both John and Marsha must embark on individual journeys into the greater intimacy of inner awareness. They must first come to know EuStillness on their own.

So that is the first step for John and Marsha to discover and become friends with their inner Selves. The more familiar you become with your own inner essence, universal love, the more you recognize it in your partner. This instruction echoes down the ancient halls of wisdom where Socrates once taught, "Know thy Self." Hopefully John and Marsha will learn what you already know – that is, how easy it is to naturally bond and become lifelong friends with EuStillness.

Once they are settled in their Selves, they have an unshakable foundation upon which to reach out and explore new worlds. They leave behind the chains of conditional love and the neurotic behaviors born of the lower needs. They no longer rely on each other to satisfy the lower security or esteem needs like money or material comfort, self-respect or confidence. Free of those binding influences, they commune with their partner from Self-love. It is a remarkable realization that breathes new and vibrant life into their relationship. The new relationship is not fear-driven. It is founded on Self-love, not selfish love, and the direct perception that, while I am still an individual with particular likes and needs and goals, my essence is no different than your essence.

If John and Marsha were to try and forge a love relationship without becoming aware of EuStillness, it would not work. They would have to rely on emotion or intellect to motivate them, to push them forward into the illusion of universal love. That would be putting the cart before the horse. You cannot work towards universal love. As Land is quick to point out, you must be pulled into the love phase. The force that impels you into love is love itself. When you become aware of EuStillness you are living in love. You know exactly what it is, by direct contact! You cannot wish or hope love into existence just as certainly as you cannot capture it with logic and analysis. Once you are living in love, like the grain of sand in pure water, you will easily know what people, places, things, or activities support love or oppose it. You see life through the eye and heart of the transcender. You are a transcender. You can never completely capture universal love with emotion or understand its intricacies, but you can live fully within its radiance as effortlessly and naturally as taking your next breath.

Once aware of their inner Selves, the transcender couple must share their essence with each other. Because universal love naturally unites, sharing their essence is spontaneous and effortless. Just as they had done in phases 1 and 2, they must work together if they are to remain together. But here is where most couples fail. They try to recapture what they had, which can never work. They must look at the future as a seething sea of probabilities; unformed potentialities open to the intuition of the moment. Unlike the predictability of a phase 2, 5-year plan, the phase 3 couple is perpetually surprised by the workings of universal love. They are pulled onward by the exuberance within and the joy of sharing and receiving unconditionally. The journey is so fulfilling that the goal becomes secondary in importance. Spontaneous manifestation of the unseen forces of fruition forever in their favor deepens their trust that everything is perfect just as it is.

Well, I think it's long past time for a direct experience of universal love which will help you unlock your heart along with your intellect. Your heart opens you to the possibilities of love or unification and your intellect decides which of the possibilities to explore. Either by itself can make mistakes, but working in tandem from the subtle realm of EuStillness they are an unbeatable team.

Here is a simple yet very effective experience that Land teaches in his seminars; we are just going to add the element of EuStillness. Here's how it goes . . .

The Healing with Universal Love Technique

- Think about a conflict that you have with someone. Think about the situation and how it came about.

- Now become aware of the feelings you have about this person.

- When the negative feelings are at their strongest grade their intensity 0–10. (0 would be no feeling and 10 would be unbearable.)

- Become aware of EuStillness (30 to 60 seconds).

- Now become aware of a time when you experienced unbounded love (30 to 60 seconds).

- Take that feeling of unbounded love and revisit your original difficulty. Only feel the love as you observe the conflict. See the conflict and feel the unbounded love. Do not try to fix the conflict, only observe it through the eyes of universal love (30 to 60 seconds).

- Again become aware of EuStillness and then universal love.

- Now revisit the situation as you did at the beginning and again grade it 0–10.

- Become aware of EuStillness and then Eufeeling …

In all likelihood you experienced a dramatic dissolution of your negative feelings. In the end you may not have been able to elicit a negative feeling at all. The situation remains, but completely free of negative feeling. Additionally, you may now be wrapped in a warm and protective blanket of universal love.

If you chose an incident with very strong emotional overtones you may have experienced the emotions getting stronger during this short session. This is normal and an example of deep emotional healing taking place. Wait a little while, a few hours is usually long enough, and repeat the EuStillness Universal Love Technique. You will be quite amazed how quickly long-standing and even deeply rooted destructive relationships will mend.

Universal love does not break boundaries, it unites them. After becoming aware of universal love, when you revisited the conflict between you and the other person the discordance immediately begins to soften and dissolve in that love. The only way for negative feelings to remain is if you were to consciously reclaim those damaging emotions as they began to dissolve. If you found yourself hanging on to the negativity, then just repeat the EuStillness Universal Love Technique again, either right away or after some time.

You and I have been through a lot together since you first opened this book. Now it's not time for us to separate just yet, but we are drawing near the end of our time together. I want to encourage you to continue to deepen your relationship ... not with me, but with your Self. I have devoted the whole next chapter to help you do exactly that. When you have finished that chapter you will know exactly how to go about establishing EuStillness in your everyday life, becoming enlightened, becoming a transcender, living in phase 3 universal love, or becoming fully human. They are all one and the same.

Main Points – Chapter 14

- The theory of transformation is a way to understand how every system in Nature evolves through three irrefutable steps.

- Nature does exactly what it should, when it should. Nature is more than reactive, it is creative.

- Universal love does not break boundaries, it unites them.

- Nothing fails like success. When doing what was once successful begins to fail, it's time to move on to the next phase.

- Perception of EuStillness gives rise to Eufeeling, the blueprint of evolution, for transition to the love phase.

- You cannot work toward universal love or wish or hope it into existence.

- EuStillness unlocks your heart and your intellect. Your heart opens you to the possibilities of love and your intellect decides which of those possibilities to explore.

- The phase 3 relationship requires a kind of letting go and trusting in the unifying force of love.

- The joy of a relationship is that its rewards are exponential.

CHAPTER 15

ON BECOMING FULLY HUMAN:

90 Days of EuStillness

"Don't aim for success if you want it; just do what you love and believe in, and it will come naturally."

~DAVID FROST

Becoming fully human is effortless once you get the hang of it. Establishing the EuStillness habit is actually easier than crafting most habits, because the feedback you get from EuStillness feels so good. However, you are learning a new skill and it does take some time to incorporate that skill into your daily routine.

Don't look at this 90-day program to establish EuStillness and become fully human like you would a weight loss or exercise program. This program only works if it is easy and if you have fun doing it. That is a major part of your job, having fun! As you already know you cannot force the perception of EuStillness. Trying to be still is an effort. An effort is activity. You cannot do the activity of stillness. Do you see what I mean? You cannot do stillness, you can only be stillness. So make it easy and make it fun.

In the beginning it takes a little conscious direction on your part to become aware of EuStillness. This will not always be the case. In fact, in a very short time you will be aware of EuStillness whenever you think of it. It's like putting on a coat on a chilly day. When you first put on the coat, you can feel its weight and warmth. After some time you forget about the coat and go about your business. But the coat is always with you, keeping you warm. Whenever you like you can have the thought, *Am I wearing my coat, and is it keeping me warm?* Immediately your awareness effortlessly shifts to your coat and you know it to be there. Then you become aware that the coat is keeping you warm. The coat is like EuStillness, and the warmth is like Eufeeling. Once your mind is accustomed to it, which could be almost immediately, it becomes aware of both the coat and the warmth at the same time. You come to know the stillness that underlies and unifies the joy of being fully human.

When you first learn the EuStillness Technique it's good to immediately begin this 90-day program to establish EuStillness in your daily routine. Becoming fully human is almost effortless and actually a lot of fun. In fact, you cannot force it or try to *make* it work. It only works if it is almost effortless. I say *almost* because, in the beginning, you must become aware enough to become *aware* of EuStillness, and this extra step requires some shift of attention from whatever you are doing to EuStillness. But you will find it fascinating. And in a very short time

(90 days or less) you will find you are living a more vivacious and successful existence.

Here is a simple illustration to point out the importance of doing the 90-Day EuStillness Program over the next 90 days. Multiply the number of years you have lived by four. If you are 45 years old, then you would multiply 45 × 4 = 180. The number 180 represents the approximate total of 90-day periods you have had in your lifetime. Imagine what you will accomplish and how much fun and excitement you will have in just one more 90-day period. Are you ready to start?

First I want to show you . . .

The EuStillness Mini-Med (Mini-Meditation) Technique

- Become aware of your whole body.
- Become aware of EuStillness in your whole body.
- Become aware of EuStillness in everything, all around you.
- Become aware of Eufeeling ...

Do the EuStillness Mini-Med Technique as often as you think about it. It takes only 2 to 4 seconds, hence the name "Mini-Med" (short for mini-meditation), so you can do it anytime there is a break in activity: between breaths, between sentences, between mouthfuls, between street signs, between thoughts, if you are a teenager between girlfriends and boyfriends. Always end with and linger awhile on Eufeeling. Eufeeling is the icing on the cake. It activates the fullness of stillness in everything you do.

This innocent technique, when done regularly, profoundly influences your outlook on life. You will begin to enjoy greater richness, balance, and appreciation in everything. If you do nothing other than just the EuStillness Mini-Med Technique, you will feel yourself being pulled quickly toward the energy of enlightenment.

Additional Activities of the 90-Day EuStillness Program

- Play with EuStillness continuously throughout the day. In the beginning you might want to place little sticky notes on your bathroom mirror, computer, car dashboard, refrigerator, and so on. What do you write on these notes? Nothing! The empty space serves to remind you that you need to do nothing but become aware of EuStillness. As you make the EuStillness Technique a "habit" you will be surprised at how soon, how often, and how effortlessly EuStillness will show up on its own.

- Adding EuStillness meditation (EuMed) to your daily routine can improve the results of the 90-Day EuStillness Program up to 1200%. Do Eu-med sitting with your eyes closed. Even though you are taking this time away from your active day, you will actually increase your energy levels, productivity, and creativity while decreasing your stress. You might think that sitting with your eyes closed is a waste of time, but nothing could be further from the truth. And, the more

regularly you do EuMed the more productive
you become. It really is most remarkable!
You can do 1 to 3 sessions a day. Best
results come when you accumulate 30 to 45
minutes per day. As an example, you could
do three 10-minute sessions, two 20-minute
sessions, or one 35-minute session, or any
combination of the three, and still realize
remarkable results. Two or three shorter
EuMed sessions are generally better than one
long one. If you like, you can work up to an
hour per day, but start with shorter times
in the beginning. Many people Eu-med just
after they wake up, before they go to sleep
at night, and somewhere in the middle of
their day, maybe at lunch or when they get
home from work, to release stress and boost
energy. Just 30 minutes of EuMed a day
will shift your EuStillness 90-Day program
into high gear and greatly accelerate your
results. (CAUTION: because of the extremely
deep rest your body and mind get during
the longer, eyes-closed EuMed session, you
must enter back into normal activity slowly
or you may experience some discomfort like
irritability or a headache. After an extended
EuStillness session, just sit and let your mind
wander for 1 to 3 minutes and then gently
become more active.)

• Every day, endeavor to do as many different
kinds of EuStillness techniques and
experiences as you can. Remember you can
do the EuStillness Healing Technique with

anything including rocks, plants, or candy bars, and don't forget you can even do it remotely. Here is a list of the techniques and experiences you have learned in this book:

1. The Nothing Technique

2. The Eufeeling Technique

3. The EuStillness Technique

4. The Stop-Hand Technique

5. The EuStillness Healing Technique

6. The Coin Technique

7. The EuStillness Decision Technique

8. The EuStillness Universal Love Technique

9. Healing with Universal Love Technique

10. The EuStillness Mini-Med Technique

11. EuMed – The EuStillness Meditation Technique

• Do the EuStillness Healing Techniques for others often. Give it away. You don't need their permission because you aren't doing anything to anyone. Just do EuStillness Healing, lots of it.

• Read a little from this book every day. You don't have to read a lot. Just a paragraph or so is enough to stimulate your intellect. Remember, knowledge is complete only when experience and understanding support each other.

• Don't look for results. Let them sneak up and surprise you. Results will begin way before your 90 days are over. But they will arrive when they are needed and where they are needed. Your body and mind will heal on a priority basis, and the best way to interfere with results is to continually look for them. Remember, transcenders live by quantum mechanical probabilities, not classical certainties. Just enjoy the EuStillness Techniques and go about your normal everyday affairs. Once you let go of control you will be amazed at how much you will accomplish.

- Slow down! At certain times of the day, make idleness a priority. When waiting, let your mind wander. Don't immediately engage your phone, a book, or any other diversion. At first you might be antsy and look for something to "do". Resist the urge. Do the Mini-Med and then just let your mind wander wherever it wants to go. The resulting creativity and release of tension will more than make up for the apparent "down time".

- Incorporate the five natural health practices into your regimen: clean air, pure water, nutritious food, sufficient exercise, and proper rest.

- Have fun and enjoy the EuStillness Techniques for what they are – a natural expression of harmonious living, of being fully human.

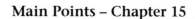

Main Points – Chapter 15

- You are learning a new skill, and it does take some time to incorporate that skill into your daily routine.

- The 90-Day EuStillness Program only works if it is easy and if you have fun doing it.

- In a very short time you will be aware of EuStillness whenever you think of it.

- Have fun and enjoy the EuStillness Technique for what it is – a natural expression of harmonious living, of being fully human.

- Becoming fully human is fun and almost effortless.

CHAPTER 16

WINNING THE HUMAN RACE:

Universal Love on the Universal Level

*"Unless someone like you cares a whole awful lot,
nothing is going to get better. It's not."*

~ DR. SEUSS

Well, it looks like we are coming to the end of our time together. I've had a great time hanging with you, hope you have as well. And I've learned a lot, too. Maybe that last statement needs a little explanation. When I write – and it may be the same for you – I am often surprised what shows up on my monitor. I write mostly from EuStillness. Maybe you felt some sense of well-being as you read through the pages and chapters of this book. I start out with a general idea of what I want to share with you, and then I just let

EuStillness flesh out the principles and examples and experiences as I write. I just love it when a crisp, new analogy pops into my mind to help explain a point I'm working on. What a joy is writing. I feel more like you, the reader, than the author of this book. I am forever discovering and then divulging secrets that lie mostly hidden from me when I am not writing. Discovering the truth that lies within is a remarkably magical process that will manifest much more readily in both our lives as we drink ever more deeply of that divine elixir, EuStillness.

We have just a few things I would like to touch on before we say goodbye. As I look back to where we started I am quite surprised at how much has happened in such a short time. Like a rags to riches story, we also started with nothing. But nothing, as it turned out, is the riches, some say humanity's greatest treasure. We learned that everything has form and energy. When form disappears, there is nothing. When energy disappears, there is stillness. We then discovered that the perception of stillness has a powerful healing effect, and that the perception of EuStillness has the greatest influence on health, harmony, and all-around quality of life. From there we were off and running.

Right from the very beginning you found out that you came into this world with everything you need to be fully human. And by direct experience you found out that you still have it. You did the Nothing Technique and found pure awareness peeking out at you from behind your thoughts. Then you did the Eufeeling Technique and found an open door to an old friend waiting with open arms. Next you dove into the silent depths of Eufeeling and discovered the unbounded, all-permeating essence of all, EuStillness. Then you learned the Stop-Hand Technique that revealed within every object, thought, and emotion, everywhere you will find EuStillness.

Perhaps most startling to many of you was the realization that simply by becoming aware of EuStillness you could inspire healing, not only within yourself but in your friends and family and even your pets. Possibly even more amazing, you discovered that you could do EuStillness healing remotely with friends next door or on the other side of the globe. When you were introduced to the Coin Technique you found that opposites like young and old, good and bad, right and wrong, all find commonality in EuStillness, reducing anxiety and resolving inner conflict. Another kind of inner conflict, the inability to determine the right course of action, was solved when you learned the EuStillness Decision Technique. From there you opened your awareness to unbounded love with the EuStillness Universal Love Technique, and later learned to heal wounded relationships when you applied the Healing with Universal Love Technique. Last, and shortest but not least, you learned the EuStillness Mini-Med Technique that keeps EuStillness and Eufeeling vibrating in your awareness all day long.

What you have in this little book is a medicine bag bulging with timely, vital remedies that can heal the ills of humankind, starting of course with yourself. (Where else could you possibly start?)

Experientially you hold in your hands a powerhouse of life-altering techniques and experiences. But no matter how vital, experience by itself is not enough. Knowledge is not complete until understanding supports that experience. It's like building a wall of bricks and mortar. The well-defined brick is like information and the formless mortar represents experience. Build your wall of bricks alone and it will topple in the first strong wind. Build it of mortar alone and you succeed in creating an amorphous mess. But, lay brick upon mortar upon brick and you create a strong, well-defined wall that will last. Along with the profound experiences laid out in this book I have also provided you with a well-defined philosophy supported by established scientific research.

Once the value of stillness was established experientially, we went on to explore the deeper, more penetrating truths that explain the dynamic effects of being still. Along the way we dispelled many common misconceptions, some of which have been with us for many generations. Early on we probed the potential of direct perception of stillness and found it to instantly impact our body and mind, eliminating the years of practice and study of most traditional "spiritual" systems. We learned that rest is the universal healer and that we experience the deepest rest when we are aware of EuStillness. We took a look at the negative side of positive thinking and eliminated the law of attraction as a reproducible scientific technique. Then we went on to establish EuStillness as the ground state connecting and supporting both negative and positive thinking and acting. We discovered that EuStillness is a reset button for negative tendencies. Becoming aware of EuStillness brings us to the ground state from which we can restructure our lives founded on love, not fear.

We took time to peruse the human condition à la Abraham Maslow and found that we are capable of living a much fuller and more fulfilling life than is commonly experienced. We looked into the qualities of transcenders and found those same potentials vibrating within us when aware of EuStillness. We found that having too many choices can be debilitating but that by taking even a momentary pause, harmony is quickly re-established. We learned that love is when two things unite to create greater harmony, and that universal love is the force that unites them. We then came to know that EuStillness is the basis of universal love, and Eufeeling is its expression. We also took a look at the theory of transformation and the three phases that every system must traverse if it is to reach its full potential. We watched John and Marsha as they evolved through the survival, expansion, and finally love phases, creating a fully human relationship in universal love.

But we are not quite done, for we have not yet shined the light of EuStillness on humanity as a whole. We humans have done a pretty good job of surviving and expanding our territory of influence to dominate this planet. But we face the same plight that John and Marsha struggled with when it was time for them to leave behind the phase 2 power practices of competition and uncontrolled growth for the softer but more potent unifying power of phase 3 love.

We know something is wrong. It is a wee tiny whisper, sometimes felt rather than heard during the quiet times. It is unsettling and unnerving and thrusts us toward more and more activity in an effort to drive out that specter of discontent. We stay busy, earning more, spending more, building more, learning more, more, more ... But the wee tiny whisper won't go away. You see, we have made a mistake. We try to fill the void with things and thoughts. Oddly enough, the emptiness we feel is eliminated when we are Eustill. Relative stillness makes it worse while absolute stillness heals it completely.

Humanity is made of what ... individuals, right? If 99% of those individuals are living in the deficiency realm of

Maslow's lower needs and Land's phases 1 and 2, then the 1% of those who are living in love constitute a very wee tiny whisper, to be sure. As a whole we humans continue to endorse phase 2 behavior and the more it fails – remember, nothing fails like success – the more vehemently we pursue those very things that are driving us to the brink of destruction.

We have work ahead of us, that is certain. We look back over a couple thousand years of our history and see that language, domestication of animals, agriculture, the building of cities, the accumulation of knowledge, the discovery of science, and the proliferation of technology played vital roles in our survival and current dominion over all other species. It is the phase 2 linear thinking that tells us that what has worked in the past will continue to work for us now, so we continue our efforts to grow and expand. Of course we now know that this thinking will be our demise.

We have been pulling in different directions, succumbing to individual desire over the good of the whole. Out of the sheer need for survival and growth, our earliest ancestors banded together in small groups and tribes. We still follow that model today. Humanity has coalesced into groups within groups, but all with their own agendas. We have become experts at surviving and growing, but to what end? We have become mesmerized by our own prowess. Growth is not a goal. It is a means to an end. And here's something that very few of us realize: We cannot continue to grow forever. Nature will not tolerate it. We have reached the saturation point where our own success is destroying us. But this is by design. It is Nature's way of leading us into the next chapter of human evolution. This is the way all life evolves, and we are no different.

We cannot return to the simpler times of our past, nor can we stay where we are. At this most precarious point, to attempt either would simply drive home the final nail in our collective coffin. We have but one choice and that is to step forward into fullness.

I stand in awe at the depth of intelligence that is behind this display of harmony, and feel deeply fortunate to be privy to its secrets, to observe creation, as it were, from the bottom up. I am forever being surprised by joy as it manifests in both the miraculous and the mundane. This deceptively simple understanding and its application of transformation – and I say this from the deepest sense of humility – may be all the knowledge we need to transcend our present peril and finally fill our potential of being fully human.

With the advent of the EuStillness Technique and recent, relevant research, we now have both the vehicle and the roadmap to reach our destination. United in cause and effect, we will leave behind the iridescent desert that has subjugated the mind and soul of humanity. We have everything we need right here, right now. The only thing holding us back is ignorance of our own full potential.

Well, I tend to get a little worked up over this issue, and I hope you will give me a pass just this once. But I do have concerns, a kind of cosmic sadness, if you will. I look around and realize our astounding potential lays fallow because we cannot rouse ourselves from so sound a slumber. I wonder if we will ever awaken. But then I realize, this too is a manifestation of the perfect order of Nature. Then I remind myself that my little slice of creation is mine to care for. When I take my own advice, when I balance my natural urge to construct and create with absolute stillness, my world flourishes in love.

You are a part of my world and I want to thank you for keeping me company as we gamboled and grew through the pages of this book. I appreciate your participation and I hope that you have found our time together interesting, if not all-out inspiring. But more than your participation, I appreciate you. You are among a small minority, perhaps a transcender or certainly on your way to becoming one, who has both the interest and the inspiration to grow in love. When you tell a friend or co-worker that you are learning to love, you might find them rolling their eyes or snickering behind your back. It won't be too long before their wee little whisper hoists a megaphone and yells in their ear, "Wake up! Something is wrong! It has been wrong for a long time and is not getting any better. It's time you learned to love." And you will be there, your wee little whisper absolutely still, and you will be doing nothing.

GLOSSARY

Enlightenment – [see EuStillness awareness] transcendence of ego; free of fear; motivated by truth, beauty, goodness, and unity; innovators, discoverers; two stages: EuAwareness (first stage), EuStillness awareness (second stage).

EuAwareness – Action performed while aware of Eufeeling. Awareness beyond the bonds of cause and effect, free of fear and disharmony. One becomes the observer as creation takes place through them, not from them.

Eufeeling – The perception of wholeness. The first glimmering of individuality in the mind. The natural state of human awareness. Eufeeling is timeless and cannot die. The mind recognizes Eufeeling as pure peace, joy, compassion, love, bliss, etc. The foundation for EuAwareness and precursor to EuStillness awareness.

EuMed – EuStillness meditation. Doing the EuStillness Technique sitting with eyes closed usually for extended periods of time. Part of the EuStillness 90-Day Program.

EuStillness – Absolute stillness. Unexpressed universal love. The lens through which pure awareness creates. The perception of Eufeeling before it takes form in the mind. (Also known as Pure Eufeeling.)

EuStillness Awareness – [see Enlightenment] the perception of pure awareness in the phenomenal world. Awareness of absolute, non-moving, undying stillness at the same time you are aware of the always changing, always moving realm of phenomenal existence. The purest state of individual awareness while thinking and acting. Being fully human.

Intuition – the quietest, subtlest, most refined reflection of Eufeeling. Thinking and feeling are conceived in the womb of intuition. A perception of wholeness, certain knowing.

Love – when two things unite to create greater harmony. The expression of order; coherence. The opposite of entropy; of death.

Non-transcender – member of any group below self-actualizing. Rarely if ever have peak experience.

Nothing – (See pure awareness) What is left when form completely dissipates.

Phase 1 – Survival: The stage of growth where the type of creativity relies on invention. The growing organism is searching for an initial pattern of successful growth that will connect with its environment.

Phase 2 – Expansion: Once a first phase pattern has been invented growth demands that creativity shift to building on a pattern, by repeating, improving, and extending it. Characterized by linear, analytical thinking. Push towards a single point.

Phase 3 – Love: A system opens to creative innovation. This requires integrating what was previously excluded and including the new and the different within the old pattern. Characterized by nonlinear, intuitive thinking. Pulled towards infinite possibilities. Transcenders exhibit phase 3, love behavior.

Pure Awareness – that which is unchanging, without beginning or end. Nothing; absolute stillness. The state of no thoughts. The gap between thoughts. Beyond form and energy. All permeating.

Self – (see Eufeeling)

Self-actualization – early stages of self-actualizing group. Peak experiences. Perceives EuAwareness.

Self-awareness – (see EuAwareness)

Stillness – (see Pure Awareness) What is left when energy stops moving.

Theory of transformation – An original interpretation detailing Nature's dynamic creative growth and change process. The three phases of growth and transformation that every system must traverse. Discovered by George Land.

Transcender – highest level in self-actualizing group. Plateau experiences Includes the self-actualizer. Experiences EuStillness. Enlightened. Phase 3, love behavior.

Universal love – the force that unites. Can only be lived through direct experience. Cannot be learned by practicing forgiveness, charity, acceptance, serenity, or the like.

FURTHER READING
AND RESOURCES

About the Kinslow System

Learn Quantum Entrainment online at: www.Kinslow
System.com

Dr. Kinslow is the originator and sole teacher of Quantum
Entrainment® and the EuStillness™ Technique. He
conducts seminars and lectures worldwide. For more
information about QE and ES, please contact us at:

Website: **www.KinslowSystem.com**

E-mail: **Info@KinslowSystem.com**

Phone: **(877) 811-5287** (toll-free in North America)

Books

The Kinslow System

The Secret of Instant Healing

The Secret of Quantum Living

Eufeeling!: The Art of Creating Inner Peace and Outer Prosperity

Beyond Happiness: Finding and Fulfilling Your Deepest Desire

Martina and the Ogre (A QE Children's Book)

Audio Books

The Secret of Instant Healing

The Secret of Quantum Living

Eufeeling! The Art of Creating Inner Peace and Outer Prosperity

Beyond Happiness

Audio Downloads

The Nothing Technique

The Eufeeling Technique

The EuStillness Technique

The Stop-Hand Technique

The EuStillness Healing Technique

The Coin Technique

The EuStillness Decision Technique

The Healing with Universal Love Technique

CDs

Kinslow System Exercises (2-CD set)

Exercises for Quantum Living (2-CD set)

Exercises for Quantum Living for Two (2-CD set)

Quantum Entrainment Exercises

Martina and the Ogre (A QE Children's Book)

DVDs

Quantum Entrainment Introductory Presentation

What the Bleep QE Video

Martina and the Ogre (A QE Children's Book) (*a Blu-Ray DVD*)

Other Services Found at www.KinslowSystem.com:

- Webinar – Quantum Entrainment Healing Webinar
- The Kinslow System Blog
- Social Networks
- The QE Quill [Free] Newsletter
- Free Downloads
- The QE Forum
- The Kinslow System Videos & Pictures
- YouTube Videos under Frank Kinslow

CPSIA information can be obtained at www.ICGtesting.com
Printed in the USA
LVOW11s2010110316

478802LV00001B/55/P